"Spaulding's book is a reminder that human interaction is a chance to bestow a gift. His storytelling ability, vulnerability, and powerful message make *The Gift of Influence* one of the most memorable books I have ever read."
—DOLF BERLE, former CEO and president of TopGolf Entertainment Group

"*The Gift of Influence* will open your heart and expand your mind regarding what is possible—your personal impact in the world. The pages overflow with deep and timeless wisdom punctuated with vulnerability and transparency. Tommy Spaulding is a gift to the world!"
—MARK MILLER, vice president of high-performance leadership of Chick-fil-A and bestselling author of *The Heart of Leadership*

"In these days when 'influencer' has become a job description, it would serve us well to remember what the word actually means and, more important, what the practice really is. Your personal influence is far greater than you think, and with this book you will expand your impact beyond what you ever thought possible. *The Gift of Influence* is a gift to us all."
—STEVE FARBER, author of *The Radical Leap, Greater Than Yourself*, and *Love Is Just Damn Good Business*

BY TOMMY SPAULDING

*The Gift of Influence*
*The Heart-Led Leader*
*It's Not Just Who You Know*

# THE GIFT OF INFLUENCE

# THE GIFT OF INFLUENCE

## Creating Life-Changing and Lasting Impact in Your Everyday Interactions

## TOMMY SPAULDING

CURRENCY

NEW YORK

Published in the United States by Currency, an imprint of
Random House, a division of Penguin Random House LLC, New York.

CURRENCY and its colophon are trademarks of Penguin Random House LLC.

Library of Congress Cataloging-in-Publication Data
Names: Spaulding, Tommy, author.
Title: The gift of influence / Tommy Spaulding.
Description: First edition. | New York: Currency, [2022]
Identifiers: LCCN 2022016191 (print) | LCCN 2022016192 (ebook) |
ISBN 9780593138632 (hardcover) | ISBN 9780593138649 (ebook)
Subjects: LCSH: Influence (Psychology) | Interpersonal relations. |
Interpersonal communication.
Classification: LCC BF774.S67 2022 (print) | LCC BF774 (ebook) |
DDC 153.8/52—dc23/eng/20220506
LC record available at https://lccn.loc.gov/2022016191
LC ebook record available at https://lccn.loc.gov/2022016192

Printed in the United States of America on acid-free paper

crownpublishing.com

2 4 6 8 9 7 5 3 1

ScoutAutomatedPrintCode

First Edition

Book design by Victoria Wong

*Dedicated to my stepson, Anthony.*
*Thank you for serving our country*
*and for being a gift in my life.*

# Contents

## Part IV: The Third *I* of Influence: Intent

## Part V: The Circle of Influence

# THE GIFT OF INFLUENCE

# Prologue

## FIFTY LETTERS

ifty-one days before my fiftieth birthday, I was on a Southwest Airlines flight bound for Denver. It was a bumpy ride, and the seatbelt sign kept flashing on. As we began our descent, we hit a patch of turbulence and the plane dropped a few hundred feet. Luggage fell, drinks spilled, passengers cried out. As a lot of people do in these situations, I started praying. Except I wasn't praying for the plane to recover—I was praying for it to crash.

I wanted to stop living. If the plane went down, my family would get a nice insurance settlement and I could have a dignified death without anyone knowing how painful my life had become. But the 737 leveled off and we landed safely in Denver. As I watched the other passengers unbuckle their seatbelts, text their loved ones, and go about their lives, I felt a terrible wave of shame. A plane crash would have solved my problems, but the other folks on the plane didn't want to die. No one's troubles are worth the lives of a hundred innocent people.

The truth is, by that moment I had lost all hope. I was unable to see the good in people; I saw only cynicism, deception, and hate. This was the result of a perfect storm of three awful situations that had collectively reached a fever pitch.

The first involved the ex-husband of my wife, Jill. When I met Jill nearly twenty years before, she was divorced with a three-year-old son, Anthony. I immediately fell in love with them both, and proposing to her remains the best decision I've ever made. When Jill and I had children of our own, I was determined that Anthony would feel equally loved. I was also determined to include his father, Mike, in our family.

At first Mike didn't like the idea of another father figure in Anthony's life, but he warmed up to me. Jill and I invited him over for birthdays and holidays. Mike and I went to hockey games with Anthony. We even vacationed together in Mexico as one big family. But as Anthony and I grew closer, Mike became verbally abusive toward me. When he began making serious threats, I called the police, and a judge granted a lifetime restraining order—his bullying had become that bad. But the damage was done, and the ordeal brought my family to the breaking point.

The second situation involved a woman I had partnered with to build a leadership development program for organizations. She was very talented, but after six months it became clear that our values did not align, and I pulled out of the business. A few months later, my closest family, friends, and clients gathered for the launch of my second book, *The Heart-Led Leader*. It was one of the happiest moments of my life—until a man walked up to me at the book-signing table to serve me papers. My former partner was coming after half of all my future book royalties and speaking fees. Her lawyer threatened to ruin me if I didn't cave. By the time I boarded that Southwest flight, the lawsuit had cost me over a hundred thousand dollars in legal fees.

Finally, while I was battling in court, I made the worst business decision of my life: I bought a sub sandwich franchise. I had a dream of hiring disadvantaged high school kids and teaching them leadership skills in the workplace. I had everything planned out—except how to actually run a sandwich shop. My store location was awful, I was chained to a long-term lease, and before long I was losing more than $10,000 per month and careening toward bankruptcy.

I was essentially living two lives. The first was as Tommy Spaulding, bestselling author who gave inspirational speeches to capacity crowds. This Tommy Spaulding was a leadership expert with an all-American family who coached everyone from Fortune 500 CEOs to high schoolers. But when the lights dimmed and the crowd went home, when the checks cleared and the music stopped, I was Tommy Spaulding, the failed sandwich maker who lived out of a suitcase. This Tommy Spaulding was getting sued for millions of dollars and traveling for work 250 days per year so he wouldn't have to give up his house or pull his kids out of private school. This Tommy Spaulding met new people and imagined all the terrible ways they would try to hurt and take advantage of him. This Tommy Spaulding taught leadership skills to thousands of people, then got on an airplane and prayed for it to crash.

The morning after that flight, I was lying in bed. It was the first time in weeks I had been home. I'm normally an early riser, but I felt so depressed I couldn't get up. My mind was stewing with all the things I had to do, all the money I had to spend on lawyers, all the people who had hurt me. Then, without warning, Jill burst into the room trailed by a dozen balloons. She threw open the curtains and brilliant sunlight spilled in. My eyes barely had time to adjust before she jumped onto the bed and blasted "Birthday" by the Beatles on a Bluetooth speaker.

"It's your birthday!" she cried as she danced on top of me. "It's your birthday!"

*Oh my God,* I thought, still half asleep. *I thought* I *was the one losing my mind.*

"Honey, my birthday isn't until August thirty-first," I croaked.

"No, Tommy," she said as Paul and John belted *They say it's your birthday / We're gonna have a good time.* "Today is exactly fifty days before your fiftieth birthday. And you're getting your first present today."

"Did you get me the Porsche?" I joked. When Jill had asked me a few months earlier what I wanted for my birthday, I'd told her a silver Porsche 911. We couldn't afford it, but cruising through Denver with the top down was literally the only way I could imagine being happy.

"No," Jill said, still hopping up and down on my legs. "I got you something much better." Then she stepped off the bed and turned down the music and handed me a handwritten letter. "As I said, there are fifty days before your fiftieth birthday. I'm going to give you one of these on each of them. Here is the first."

I felt a stone in the pit of my stomach as I recognized the elegant penmanship. It was from my mother. She and I had a good but challenging relationship when I was growing up. My mom loved me deeply, but she had a unique way of showing it. She ruled the house with an iron fist and gave me more chores than all my friends had combined. One thing I couldn't stand was that after my birthday parties, she'd dump a stack of blank paper on the table. "Now write a thank-you note to every person who was here today," she'd demand. I had big Italian Catholic birthdays as a child, so there were dozens and dozens of letters to write. She would proof each one, and if any seemed generic or lacked heart, I had to rewrite them.

But now, decades later, she was writing me a letter on my

birthday. It was the most beautiful thing I had ever read. She told me how much she loved me. She told me how proud she was of the difference I was making in the world and all the lives I had changed. I read and reread that letter and cried harder each time. Finally I looked up at Jill, who was crying too. "Happy birthday, sweetie," she said.

On each of the next forty-nine days, Jill gave me another letter. My friend Byron thanked me for changing the lives of his two sons. My literary agent, Michael, told me that he is nicer to people because of my influence. My mentor Jerry told me that he loved me like a son. My HVAC technician, Russ, wrote that I'd taught him how to love deeply. And on and on and on. People telling me not just how much they loved me but how much I had *influenced* them. How I had helped them become better sons, daughters, parents, spouses, bosses. How I had taught them to lead and inspired them to serve others. Now, in my darkest hour, they were influencing me with their beautiful letters. And they saved my life.

With each passing day, with each letter, the fog lifted. My three terrible problems seemed more manageable. The lawyers less nasty. My depression less deep. I was no longer the man who stepped on a plane and prayed for it to crash. Jill might not have given me a silver Porsche for my fiftieth birthday, but she had given me something infinitely more important.

She gave me the gift of influence.

# 80,000

Imagine this scene: Many years from now, after you pass away surrounded by your loved ones, you slip into the hazy twilight between life and death. You're not in heaven yet, but on the sideline of a massive stadium. For me, it's Empower Field at Mile High in Colorado, home of the Denver Broncos. For you, maybe it's Lambeau Field in Green Bay, Wisconsin; MetLife Stadium in East Rutherford, New Jersey; Notre Dame Stadium in Indiana; Beijing's National Stadium; or London's Wembley Stadium. The venue is at max capacity: eighty thousand people. But those people are not there to watch a sporting event. They are all there to say goodbye to you.

The crowd murmurs and rises to its feet as you approach midfield. Many of the faces are those of people you know: friends, family, neighbors, co-workers. But the rest you only dimly recognize: former clients and employees, friends of friends, classmates, your electrician, your daughter's basketball coach, the mailperson. These are the transactional relationships in your life that you rarely think about. The people who don't remember your name but remember how you treated them. Will these eighty thousand people be stomping, clapping, and chanting your name to thank you for the positive influence you've had on their lives? Or will they be silent? Even worse, will the crowd boo and curse your name?

Here's an even more important question: If you knew, right now, that every person you'd ever influenced would be waiting for you in a stadium at the end of your life, how would it affect you today? Would you lead and love differently? Would you treat people a little differently? Maybe a lot differently?

A few years ago, my nonprofit youth program, the National Leadership Academy, hosted our annual Book-n-Benefit fundraiser. We always feature a keynote speech by a bestselling author, and that year we'd invited my friend Jon Gordon, author of *The Energy Bus, The Power of Positive Leadership,* and other bestselling books. I love this man, and I'm among the millions who read his books religiously. Jon is a dynamite speaker, and like the rest of the audience that day, I was hanging on his every word.

At the end of his speech, Jon said something that moved me deeply: "I heard about a recent study showing that the average person will influence eighty thousand people in their lives, positively or negatively."

I felt everything go quiet as the words sank in. *We influence eighty thousand people in our lives.* I started doing the math in my head. If you divide eighty thousand by the average life expectancy—seventy-eight years—you get 1,025 people impacted per year, or 2.8 daily. Every single day, two or three people are filtering into your stadium and preparing to cheer you on, boo you off the field, or sit there trying to figure out who you are. You can choose to be a good influence, or you can choose to be a bad one. It's that simple. Will your stadium be filled with eighty thousand cheers, or jeers? The choice is yours. The eighty thousand people in your stadium won't remember how you managed or led them. They won't remember what products you sold or the services you provided. They will simply remember your actions and words that changed their lives—your legacy of influence.

In its most basic sense, influence means having a lasting effect on the character or behavior of another person. Put another way, the people with the loudest stadiums, those thumping arenas where even the folks in the nosebleed seats are stomping their feet and screaming, are the very best *influencers*. I don't blame you if that word makes you cringe. Go ahead and google the word "influencer" and see what comes up. The top hits are sites like "Influencer marketing," "The biggest influencers on TikTok," and "How to make money being a social media influencer." The word wasn't even added to the dictionary until 2019: "A person with the ability to influence potential buyers of a product or service by promoting or recommending the items on social media."

In other words, being an influencer is all about making money by getting other people to buy stuff. Yeah, it's not exactly the most inspiring message in the world. Maybe if you're one of the Kardashians you will have a stadium full of folks who bought products because of your Instagram posts. But for the rest of us, being an influencer means something much more personal.

One of the greatest influencers I know is my wife, Jill. When I'm in her stadium one day cheering furiously, I'm not going to be thinking about how she influenced me to sign up for the Marriott Vacation Club. I'll be thinking about how she saved my life with her fifty letters. Truth is, "influence" has become a negative word. It's associated with manipulating people, with getting them to do something that benefits you. While it's easy to blame Kylie Jenner, Dwayne "The Rock" Johnson, and other social media stars who are paid millions of dollars to post about tequila, the word "influence" was debased long before Instagram was invented.

The quintessential book about influence is *How to Win Friends and Influence People* by Dale Carnegie. Since it was published in 1936, the book has sold more than thirty million copies and is ranked number 19 on *Time* magazine's list of the one hundred most influential books. I've talked a lot about how Dale Carnegie changed my life, how his book got me to send handwritten notes, ask meaningful questions, avoid unnecessary conflict, and connect with people. I cherished *How to Win Friends and Influence People* and still do, but as I matured, I started reading it more closely. For instance, here are some of the chapter titles: "Increase Your Popularity," "Help You to Win People to Your Way of Thinking," "Enable You to Win New Clients, New Customers," and "Increase Your Earning Power." Carnegie even teaches us how to "let the other person feel like the idea is his or hers." Do you see a pattern?

It's all about *you*.

Do you think the eighty thousand people in your stadium will remember how you successfully won them over to your way of thinking? Probably not. They'll be cheering because you helped them become better parents, spouses, siblings, managers, and leaders. They'll remember how you inspired them to become better human beings. They'll remember the times when you loved and served them. They will be cheering because you authentically invested in them. It took me half a lifetime to understand that it's not what you can *get* out of those eighty thousand people—it's what you *give* to those eighty thousand people.

In my first book, *It's Not Just Who You Know,* I discuss the importance of building genuine and lasting relationships. I share how investing unselfishly in the lives of others is the most important thing we can do for ourselves, our organizations, our communities, and our world. In my second book, *The Heart-Led Leader,* I discuss how authentic leaders live and lead from the heart, and how they serve others before themselves. But in the years since, I've struggled with a few burning questions: What specific skills do leaders need in order to have a life-changing impact? What habits do they practice daily? What decisions do we subconsciously make day in and day out that have an outsize impact on others? Finally, and most important, what is a leader's greatest legacy?

The answer to that last question, as you probably guessed, is influence. Now, it's easy to define bad influence. You've probably had a boss or two who tried to influence you through dominance and manipulation. These people rely on fear and intimidation to get what they want. On the other hand, you may have had that boss who always recognized your efforts, never threw you under the bus, and invested in your career. In school, maybe there was a teacher who gave you a second chance after a bad grade, or who always made learning fun. Or a friend who always showed up for you during your toughest moments.

Some influencers may be CEOs, coaches, and presidents, but most lead quieter lives. They build authentic relationships and give without expecting anything in return. They constantly ask themselves, "How can I be of service today?" I've had the good fortune of meeting thousands of influencers in my life, the vast majority of whom you've never heard of. I've known influencers of many races, genders, and sexual orientations. They come from different countries. Some vote Democratic and some vote Republican. They live in the heartland and in big cities. They have almost nothing in common except four core traits: the ability to **Lift**, **Embrace**, **Act**, and **Devote** themselves to others—in other words, to **LEAD**.

Over the next four chapters, I'm going to tell you four stories about four exceptional people who embody those qualities: a junior high school math teacher, a nine-year-old hockey player, a gang leader, and a Catholic nun. I can't think of four people who are less alike, except in their ability to lead and inspire others through the power of positive influence. After that, we'll dig further into what it means to LEAD others. This means getting at the heart of influence itself: interest, investment, and intent, or what I call "the three *i*'s of influence."

Here's my promise to you: If you commit to living a life of positive influence, you will never look at your personal and professional relationships the same way again. If you commit to building a culture of influence in your teams and within your organizations, you will witness unprecedented results and success. You will end every day knowing you've changed someone's life for the better. And as I found out in the fifty days before my fiftieth birthday, when you are down for the count, when life has dealt you lemons, the very same people you've influenced along the way will lift you up and lead you home.

As I've come to learn, leadership is not about influence. Leadership *is* influence. The eighty thousand people you'll meet throughout your lifetime will be either better or worse because of the positive or negative influence you've had on them. The choice is yours. Read on—we are going on a journey to begin filling your stadium, one changed life at a time.

# PART I

# Influencers LEAD

# Lift: Thirty-six Pieces of Paper

Have you ever heard an unforgettable story—one that you can't stop thinking about for days, months, or even years? These kinds of stories aren't just heartwarming; they make us fundamentally rethink our assumptions. They change the way we see and treat other people. They change the way we live and lead.

I am about to tell you one of those stories. When I heard it for the first time, everything seemed to go still, as if time itself had slowed its relentless march just to ensure I heard about a junior high school teacher named Ms. Lynn. With one simple class exercise on a bright spring day, she taught a roomful of eighth graders that no matter how alone they might feel, however dark and cold life may get, they are loved.

There isn't a Hollywood movie about Ms. Lynn. I guarantee you've never heard of her. But Ms. Lynn's story moved me more than any movie or book ever has because it beautifully illustrates the simple and awesome power of lifting others up. That, at its heart, is what influence is all about. It's not telling people how great they are; it's *showing* them how great they are. Lifting others up means identifying moments—regardless of how insignificant they may seem—to show that they matter.

After you read about Ms. Lynn, I challenge you to slow down. Slow down as you live your day-to-day life. Slow down as you interact with your co-workers, slow down when you have dinner with your family, slow down when you're ordering food at a restaurant. Slow down and be aware of the people around you and ask yourself: How can I lift them up, even just a little bit?

**On a warm and** sunny Friday in March 1962, a thirty-year-old teacher named Ms. Lynn walked into her eighth grade math class. It was the last period of the day before spring break officially began, and Ms. Lynn took a moment to read the energy of the room.

Now, imagine you're back in eighth grade. Your mind isn't too focused on geometry to begin with. But at three o'clock on the first beautiful afternoon after a long, cold winter? Only fifty minutes before the beginning of a weeklong vacation? Forget it.

Ms. Lynn watched two boys having a wrestling match and three girls passing notes in the third row. In the corner was a girl rubbing her puffy red eyes. Her name was Betty, and Ms. Lynn knew her parents were in the middle of a divorce. The rest of the class gazed anxiously out the window, hoping to enjoy a brief glimpse of spring. She looked down at her lesson plan: the Pythagorean theorem. There was no way the class would be absorbing $A^2+B^2=C^2$ and why it was important to calculate the hypotenuse of a right triangle. Most teachers would plow ahead with the lesson anyway. But Ms. Lynn wasn't like most teachers.

After settling down the wrestlers and telling the girls to put their notes away, she removed a page from a three-ring binder and held it up to the class. "See this piece of paper? This is my lesson plan for today." Thirty-six pairs of eyes stared at it blankly, and then back out the window. With a slight smile, Ms. Lynn tore it up and tossed the fragments into the trash. The class erupted into applause. Even Betty, still fighting back tears, had a little smile on her face.

"Here's what we are going to do today," Ms. Lynn continued. "Everyone take out a piece of paper and a pencil." She had their attention now. The wrestlers, the note passers, Betty— everyone rummaged around in their desks. In the meantime, Ms. Lynn wrote the first name of each student on the blackboard.

"On the left side of your paper, I want you to do what I'm doing. List the first name of everyone in the class."

There was a flurry of scribbling, a buzz of excited energy. Something was very different about this lesson.

"Okay," Ms. Lynn said when their pencils were silent. "Now, next to each name, I want you to write one word or phrase that sums up what you love or like or admire or respect or appreciate about that person. Something positive that you've noticed about them. Got it?"

Thirty-six heads nodded vigorously and once more there was a flurry of pencils. The wrestlers stared at the page, occasionally popping their heads up to scrutinize the next person on the list. The note passers scribbled faster than their brains could think, pausing frequently to swipe eraser dust from the paper. Even Betty's eyes seemed less red as she considered each of the names and wrote what she admired about them with her looping penmanship. For the first time in the history of Ms. Lynn's period five math class, there wasn't a single peep for fifty minutes. When the bell rang, the students raced to finish their lists and Ms. Lynn sent them on their way, free at last to enjoy spring break.

During her vacation, this is what Ms. Lynn did at home: She took out thirty-six pieces of blank paper, and at the top of each one she wrote the name of one eighth grader from her class. Then she inserted the praise that had been written about them. That's 1,260 separate messages to organize and record. It took her all week.

On the Monday after spring break, Ms. Lynn's students returned, tanned and with fresh scrapes and bruises from a week of adventures. When class started, she handed each student their list. She watched their faces as they read what their peers had written. Some giggled. Some blushed. There were a few tears, even among the boys. But all were beaming.

And then the exercise was over. Ms. Lynn returned to her lesson plan on calculating the hypotenuse of a right triangle. The students stuffed into their book bags the pieces of paper their math teacher had so carefully prepared. Their eyes wandered back to the window, and they thought about crushes, friends, sports, summer vacation, and everything else on the mind of a typical eighth grader. Before long it was the end of the school year and Ms. Lynn's students had moved on to high school.

Some years passed. This was now the late 1960s in America, with the Vietnam War in full swing. By 1968 more than half a million Americans were fighting in the jungles against a new kind of enemy that used guerrilla tactics and booby traps. Soldiers trudged through rivers and swamps and all sorts of hell, not knowing when the next attack would come, who would be the next to be picked off by a sniper, who would be the next to trip a landmine.

Ms. Lynn was grading papers on her couch one day when

the phone rang. The woman on the other end was barely keeping it together. She explained that her son Mark had been killed during the battle of Khe Sanh while defending a military base from the North Vietnamese army. They would be honored if she would join them at the funeral. Ms. Lynn searched her memory and finally remembered Mark: He was one of the wrestlers from her old fifth period math class. She sat on her couch, stunned. It seemed like yesterday that Mark was goofing off at his desk, a twinkle in his eye, the faintest whisper of a mustache above his lip, the rest of his life in front of him. And now he was gone.

Ms. Lynn went to the funeral and stood for a long time outside the church, gazing at the photos of Mark on display. There was a portrait of him in his dress uniform. He looked dashing, much bigger than the boy she remembered, but the same smile was there. After the service, Mark's parents invited Ms. Lynn to their house, where they were hosting a small celebration of his life. Upon arriving, she recognized other members of her fifth period class: there were the other wrestler, the note passers, and even Betty, who had made it through her parents' divorce and grown into a strong young woman. Ms. Lynn stood awkwardly in the corner. Most of these people had known Mark intimately for years; they told story after story about his kindness, his intelligence, and his bravery. She felt embarrassed. She had barely known him; what kind of influence could she possibly have passed on?

Then Mark's father approached her. "Come with me. I'd like to show you something." He led her out of the living room, down the hallway, and into a small bedroom adorned with posters of rock 'n' roll bands and sports legends. It was Mark's room. On the small desk sat some books, old photos, and Little League trophies. The twin bed in the corner was still covered with a neatly spread Nebraska Cornhuskers comforter. But there was one item sitting in the middle of the bed that did not belong to a child: an infantryman's green camouflage helmet. A cold instrument of war surrounded by the fading memories of childhood innocence.

Mark's dad picked up the helmet and turned it over. From behind one of the straps, he extracted a yellowed, sweat-stained, scotch-taped piece of paper that must have been folded and refolded thousands of times.

"Here," he said, handing her the paper. "We found this inside his helmet. It was with him when he was killed. Open it."

Hands trembling, she carefully unfolded the fragile page. Even though years had passed, she knew instantly what it was. At the top of the page, she recognized a name written in her own script: "Mark." Below it was a list of thirty-five words and phrases: "Funny," "Kind eyes," "Always says hi to me," "Good guy," "Best quarterback." On and on and on. Ms. Lynn read them once, twice, three times. Finally she looked up, eyes welling.

A tall, strapping young man stepped into the room. It was Mark's best friend—the other wrestler. "I still have my list too," he said. "It's in the top drawer of my desk at home."

A young woman stepped into the room—one of the note passers. "Mine's in my wedding album now," she sobbed.

Then Betty came forward, reached into her purse, and pulled out a tattered piece of paper. "Ms. Lynn, there were times that year when I read this piece of paper every night before I went to bed. Thank you."

Ms. Lynn stood next to Mark's bed and looked at the faces of the people crowded around her: Mark's mother and father, Betty, and the other students from her eighth grade math class.

With one thoughtful gesture on a lazy Friday before spring break, she had fundamentally changed thirty-six lives.

Ms. Lynn sat on the bed and suddenly realized she was more than just an eighth grade math teacher. For the first time since she'd gotten that terrible phone call from Mark's mother, she put her head in her hands and wept.

# Embrace: The Captain

Like any parent, I adore my children. I have to catch myself or else I'll brag about them nonstop. That's especially true when it comes to my son Tate, who is one of the top hockey players in the country in his age group. One of the biggest joys of my life has been watching Tate be so purely and perfectly in his element while on the ice.

For most of his young life, I thought that what made Tate extra special was his ability to outskate players twice his size and make impossible slap shots look easy. I learned how wrong I was not long after my son turned nine, when a boy named Tristan joined the practice squad of Tate's traveling hockey team. While the other players instantly saw a target, Tate's reflex was to embrace Tristan and show everyone around him what leadership truly looks like.

Tate demonstrated to me the simple courage of embracing others for who they are. It sounds like such a simple concept, but very few of us are good at it. When we see someone in pain, especially a stranger, our instinct is to look away instead of looking to help. Embracing also means seeing and valuing someone for more than the service they provide for you. In an era when we cut people out of our lives because of what they look like, what church they attend or don't attend, what they post on social media, or whom they voted for, the ability to embrace another person fully and without question is very rare.

As you read through this story, I challenge you to think about the people in your life you instinctively push away. The people who are tough to love. The people you write off because they are different. What if we could simply love and embrace them, even if we don't always "click"? There is so much we can learn from influencers like Tate, if only we open our hearts.

**Tate was born with** a hockey stick in his hands. It's his passion—or, rather, his obsession. At the age of nine, he was getting up at five to practice hockey before school. Jill and I tell our friends that Tate skates better than he walks, and we're only half joking. When he was younger, instead of having us read him picture books at bedtime, Tate insisted that we recite Wayne Gretzky's career NHL records.

"Now I know all the records I'm going to break," he'd say after we were finished. So, yeah, "obsession" is the right word to use when it comes to Tate's love of hockey.

Years ago, just after Tate turned nine, I was driving him to the hockey rink at some ungodly hour when he asked me: "Daddy, what does it take to become a captain?"

In my half-awake state, I replied: "To be captain, Tate, you don't have to be the best player. You have to be the best *person*. The captain has the greatest heart on the team, but, more important, has the greatest influence on their teammates. Being a captain means embracing your weakest teammates and helping them become the strongest."

Tate stayed quiet as he soaked all that in. Finally he said: "Well, I want to be captain one day." It was a quiet, defiant tone—the kind you rarely hear from someone so young.

Tate didn't play for your ordinary town or county league. He played for an elite club in Colorado called the Krivo School of Hockey. Krivo stands for Andrei Krivokrasov, a former Red Army hockey champion from Russia who runs the program. His brother, Sergei, played ten seasons in the NHL. It's safe to say that Andrei knows a thing or two about hockey, and his program is as old-school as they come. Discipline. Practice. And more discipline. Tate, who has been playing at an elite level since he could walk, thrives in an environment like that.

Most of the kids at the Krivo School of Hockey were as gifted as Tate, but one day a boy named Tristan showed up. Let's just say that he wasn't the most talented player on the team, and everyone knew it. Tristan was not good enough to make the traveling team, so he played on the practice squad as a goalie. Many of the kids teased Tristan mercilessly and made it clear that he was not part of the tribe.

Except for one.

Tate knew that Tristan wasn't very good, but he didn't care. He saw that Tristan came to practice every single day and worked his tail off. He took his reps against the top talent in Colorado, and with a hard-ass Russian challenging him and pushing him to his limits, Tristan got his spirit crushed every day and still showed up the next morning. The other players saw a kid who should probably join the chess team; Tate saw someone he admired.

The two became friends. Tate never stopped encouraging him, always offering a high five after a save, sitting next to him in the locker room, and hanging out with him after practice.

Most important, Tate took time to learn his story. It turned out Tristan was lucky to be alive, let alone play hockey.

When Tristan was three, he experienced a grand mal seizure—that's when you lose consciousness and have violent muscle contractions. The doctors thought it was a one-time occurrence, but two months later Tristan suffered another and then another. He was prescribed a battery of medications, but the seizures continued—literally thousands per day. At age four, Tristan was placed into a medically induced coma, just to give his fragile body time to recover from the unending trauma. At the hospital, Tristan's mother, Debra, could not speak to him, could not sing to him, could not touch him, could not soothe him, for fear of triggering another onslaught of seizures. He spent months at a time in treatment—months that he should have spent going to school, making new friends, playing sports, just being a normal kid. Finally he was diagnosed with Doose Syndrome, a rare disorder that accounts for just 1 percent of all childhood-onset epilepsies. When Tristan miraculously woke up from the coma, the seizures were gone for good, but he had lost all use of his muscles. He had to relearn to move his limbs, to walk, even to eat.

When Tristan stepped onto the ice rink at the Krivo School for the first time, he was physically years behind his peers. He was lucky to be skating at all, let alone defending slap shots by boys twice his size. The other players didn't see it that way. They laughed at him, knocked him down, called him names. But the meaner they were, the more loving Tate became.

Toward the end of the season, Debra called me and asked, "Can you send me all the Saturday afternoons your son has available this month?"

"Sure . . . why?" I asked, a little confused.

"We are planning Tristan's birthday party, and he wants to make sure Tate can make it."

I was stunned—who arranges a birthday party around one kid's schedule?

The week after the party, Debra approached me at hockey practice. She had tears in her eyes. "I just wanted you to know that we invited a few kids from the hockey team, but Tate was the only one who came. You have no idea how much of an impact your son has had on Tristan. Tate is always building him up. What a special kid you have."

A few weeks later, I picked Tate up from hockey practice. He had a huge smile on his face.

"Daddy, guess what?" he said. "Coach Krivo named me captain of the team!"

I stared at him. In all Andrei's years coaching the traveling team, he had famously never named a captain. Until now.

I started to cry. I told Tate that in his nine years, I'd never been prouder of him. "Remember when you asked me what it means to be a captain?" I said. "It's not about being the best player; it's about being the best person. You helped the weakest player on your team realize he was strong. In my book, Tate, you just broke all of Wayne Gretzky's records."

# Act: The Gang Leader

"Nothing happens until something moves," Albert Einstein once said. All of us have things we would do, wrongs we would right, if only we had the time. But then life gets in the way, time marches on, and things we ought to do become things we ought to have done.

And then there are people, like George Taylor, who simply act. When he heard about a horrific gang-related shooting in his hometown, George acted. But here's what makes him extra special: His solution wasn't to try to eradicate street gangs but to study them, understand them, learn from them, and then help them. What George did next is one of the most inspiring stories I have ever heard, one that reveals the power of community, love, and beer.

George's story inspired me to reflect on my own actions and inactions, on the times I failed to act at all and the times I failed to act wisely. I thought about how sometimes life boils down to the actions we take—or don't take—when it matters most. As you read this story, I ask you to do the same. Reflect on what it means not just to act but to act with compassion, positive intent, and love.

———

**George Taylor was listening** to the radio in Wilmington, North Carolina, when the news broke: A sixteen-year-old boy had been killed in a drive-by shooting just blocks from his downtown office. George was shocked to hear that the shooting was gang-related. As an affluent businessman who lived in a gated community, he didn't even realize there were gangs in Wilmington. It's a prosperous tourist city nestled between the Cape Fear River and the Atlantic Ocean. It's not the kind of place you usually see on crime shows.

When most people hear about tragedies like this, they shake their heads and complain that someone ought to do something about it. Then they change the channel and get back to their dinner.

Not George Taylor.

At first, he was angry that this kind of violence could happen in his hometown. George had helped launch numerous tech start-ups in Wilmington, including Untappd, the largest online beer social networking community in the world. But he didn't just want to stop gang violence; he wanted to fundamentally understand why someone would drive down the street, stick a pistol out the window at another person, and pull the trigger. So George called up the district attorney and asked for a sit-down with the top gang leader in the city.

Yeah, my mouth fell open when I heard that too.

The DA was understandably skeptical of George's plan. A white tech entrepreneur in his late fifties who knew nothing about street gangs wanted to meet a black gangster who had almost certainly been involved in numerous murders. But George is persistent, and a few weeks later the DA agreed to connect him with Bill, a high-ranking member of the Bloods, the notorious street gang formed in Los Angeles in the early 1970s. Bill was out on parole and might be willing to sit down with George, but there was one problem: Bill suspected this was an elaborate sting operation and refused to meet him without a lawyer present.

Here's the message George sent back: "You tell Bill that if he doesn't have the balls to meet me one on one, man to man, then he can go fuck himself and I'll find somebody else who will."

A week later, Bill showed up—alone.

He told George what it really meant to be in a gang, and the conversation changed George's life. TV and movies often give the impression that street gangs appeal to lowlifes who love dealing drugs and committing violence. That's certainly what I thought for most of my life. In fact, the opposite is true. Like corporations, organized street gangs have written key values and vision statements detailing what they stand for, what they believe in, and what they're trying to build. In these mission statements, there was nothing about drugs, guns, or drive-by shootings. Instead, George recognized values like community, growth, knowledge, brotherhood, and loyalty. When violence does occur, Bill explained, it's primarily driven by economic challenges and societal exclusion. Often young men are considered unemployable because of how they look or talk, or because of prior convictions for minor offenses. They fall through the cracks. When these men and their families are banished to crumbling and underserved housing projects, some resort to the kinds of activities we associate with gangs because there are few other choices.

After speaking with Bill, George spent nearly three years traveling the country to learn about gangs. He talked with Bloods and Crips in Los Angeles, Vice Lords in Atlanta, and GD in Chicago. He spoke with and gained the trust of gang members at all levels of the hierarchy and learned how these organizations help lift urban communities that have long since been left behind. George soon understood that the answer to curbing gang violence wasn't getting rid of gangs but offering inclusive economic opportunity. Then he had an idea: What if he could create a company—not some charity, but a bona fide for-profit corporation—that employed active gang members? As chairman of Untappd, the answer was staring George right in the face: a brewery.

In October 2019, George bought an abandoned fifty-eight-thousand-square-foot textile mill in Wilmington and spent more than a year renovating it. Then came the most important step: hiring staff. Most companies let you apply over job sites like Indeed or Monster. George handles things a little differently. First, to work for him, you must be an active gang member. Second, all applicants must attend a two-month boot camp called DisruptU, where they learn everything from marketing to branding to brewing. Most important, they are counseled to break free of the limiting beliefs so many of them grew up with, such as believing they cannot be happy or successful because they grew up in the wrong zip code, attended the wrong school, or have the wrong skin color.

If you are late for DisruptU, even once, you're let go and can reapply in ninety days. At the end of boot camp, you're initiated into the brewery business by jumping out of an airplane—no small feat, considering many of these men have never been on an airplane, let alone jumped out of one with a parachute. When you start boot camp you're provided a salary of $30,000 and health insurance. Anyone who makes it through boot camp receives a raise to $35,000, which increases to a minimum of $37,500 after ninety days. After that, you start getting stock options. Not bad for guys whose gang associations meant they could previously only get minimum-wage gigs flipping burgers, if they were lucky.

But here's the truly crazy part: During boot camp, George takes the gang members who hate one another the most—think Bloods and Crips—and pairs them up. These aren't minor feuds, like dinging a car or stealing a few bucks; some of the guys in that room have shot or stabbed the man next to him. Take Steve and Dune—two men from two different sides of town. Steve was a Blood, Dune was GD. Years earlier, the rival gangs got into an argument. Dune's best friend pulled out a knife and stabbed Steve. He survived, but when the two gangs met again and started brawling, Steve shot Dune's friend dead. Steve took a plea deal and spent two years in prison, then spent another ten years bouncing between dead-end jobs trying to support his family. What reputable company would hire a felon, let alone a convicted murderer? Then he met George Taylor.

When Steve showed up for boot camp, he was sitting next to none other than Dune. At first, they were ready to strangle each other, but the instructors were prepared and managed to coax them through boot camp. Little by little, the tensions subsided, as they began to see how much they had in common. They had the same dreams and the same struggles. Before long they became friends and were sharing Thanksgiving turkey. Steve and Dune's story later helped inspire the brewery's name, TRU Colors: Beer Without Rival.

There certainly have been hiccups along the way. When Press, an active Bloods gang leader, was arrested on a weapons charge, George had to let him go. The brewery has a strict no-guns policy. The next day, George received a text from Press asking to talk. When they met up, George saw that he was in rough shape. Press had been sleeping in his car and had nowhere else to go. George sized up the situation and decided Press had hit rock bottom and was ready for a change.

"I can't hire you back because of the outstanding weapons charge," George said, "but I'll let you live with us at my house." Press moved in that night with George and his wife, and when George woke up the following morning and came into the living room, his mouth fell open: Press had cut off his shoulder-length dreadlocks and shaved his head.

"I'm ready to change," he said, "and I want you to know I mean it." Later that week, George made a call and found Press a job working construction.

August in North Carolina is not pleasant. Press spent grueling ten-hour days jackhammering concrete in hundred-degree temperatures, but he never complained. When his court date rolled around eight months later, George wrote a letter to the DA describing Press's transformation. When the DA offered Press a deal with no jail time, George gave him his old job back at TRU Colors, and he spent the next three years studying brewing operations. Today, Press is a brewer at TRU Colors. He owns a house. He has a family. And he knows how to make a killer IPA.

George told me about all of this when he invited me to speak at the brewery in early 2021. TRU Colors was putting the finishing touches on their operation before beginning mass production and distribution later that summer. Even though I've given thousands of keynote addresses, I've never been more nervous than the day I spoke at TRU Colors.

Before my speech I met a young man with long dreadlocks and the word THUG tattooed down his throat. That was his street name, he said matter-of-factly. Thug was a high-status member of GD in North Carolina. A few months earlier he had been in a car with his best friend, Nas, when another vehicle screeched to a halt beside them. Four men jumped out with guns and began firing. The windows exploded as bullets rained inside the car. Thug threw himself down. All he could hear were screams and the sound of cartridge shells falling to the pavement. He looked up just as two bullets hit Nas in the head. With shots still flying, Thug crawled into the driver's seat, got control of the car, and sped to the hospital with Nas's head in his lap. Tragically, Nas died on the way. Now, three months later, here I was about to speak to Thug about love and servant leadership.

*What the hell am I doing here?* I thought. What on earth could a white boy from the suburbs of Denver possibly say to men who have seen their friends and family gunned down? When I stood up to address the thirty or so employees, they watched me politely. I looked down at my notes about heart-led leadership and the usual stories I told about growing up dyslexic. My academic struggles seemed so insignificant compared to what these men had endured just to be here today. So I set aside my notes and decided to tell a story I had never told anyone before.

"I was ready to kill someone once," I said. My mouth went dry as I said the words. Until then I hadn't really believed them myself.

I took a deep breath and told my audience of Bloods, Crips, and GD about the newspaper route I kept when I was fourteen years old in Suffern, New York. I knew all the families on my route except one. It was a house at the end of the cul-de-sac on Marian Drive. Every Sunday the man who lived there would leave an envelope under his doormat. Inside was $2.25 for the newspaper and a twenty-five-cent tip for me. I never met the man, but every Sunday he left the same envelope with the same tip.

A few days after the *Journal News* raised its price to $2.50, I knocked on the man's door. An older gentleman opened it and I thanked him for his generosity. If he wanted to keep tipping, I explained, he needed to add another quarter to the envelope going forward. Then he asked if I went to school nearby.

"Yes, at Suffern Junior High School," I said.

"Do you play sports?"

"I'm on the wrestling team."

"That's great. I love wrestling. I'd like to teach you some moves. Do you want to go in the backyard and practice?"

I hesitated. The man looked friendly enough. He always gave me a tip. He was an adult, and I was a fourteen-year-old paperboy who had seen so very little of the world. I agreed, and we went around back and began to wrestle. And then he molested me. He was the first person ever to touch me in that way. I kicked him off before he could go further and sprinted home to tell my parents. It was a different time back then, and these matters were handled differently than how they are now. My parents approached the leaders of our church, who said they would handle it. But they never did. I later tracked down the three previous paperboys on that route, and they all admitted that the man had tried to touch them too. I felt embarrassed that I had been so naïve. I thought it was my own fault for being too trusting.

I wasn't old enough to process what had happened to me, and I never spoke about it again. In a way, I never truly processed it until that day at the TRU Colors brewery. In high school and college, I was consumed by shame and anger. During my sophomore year of college, the hurt became unbearable. While home for spring break, I grabbed a baseball bat and drove to the house at the end of my old paper route. I walked up to the front door, gripping the bat so hard my knuckles were white. Then I rang the doorbell, ready to beat the piss out of the man who had stolen my adolescence.

Instead, an old woman opened the door. The previous owner had moved away some years before, she said. As she closed the door, I felt the adrenaline burn like acid through my insides, slowly dissipating until I felt hollowed out. I dropped the bat and broke down crying.

"If that man had not moved away, I would not be standing here today," I said. The room was deathly quiet. "I would have hurt him. I might have killed him."

Suddenly I felt lighter, as if a five-hundred-pound weight had been lifted off my chest. I scanned the faces of my confessors—the Bloods, Crips, and GD I had chosen to tell this story to for the first time in my life. Men who had beaten and killed other people. Men who had done unspeakable things. And yet, as I looked them in the eye, I felt a brotherhood. They understood me and I understood them. Many had endured hell because they lost the birth lottery and grew up on the cold streets instead of in a warm home. In many ways I live a charmed life. I have a fulfilling career and a wonderful family. But I'd have none of that if fate had worked a little differently and my abuser had answered the door instead of an old woman.

Fate had worked differently for the gang members in my audience. I was given a single chance to screw up my life; they were given a lifetime of chances. Yet somehow they'd found their way to this brewery. In that moment I understood what made TRU Colors so special. It was run by people like Steve, Press, Dune, and Thug—men to whom life had never given a first chance, let alone a second one. But they decided to act, and by so doing they changed their circumstances through sheer force of will. They acted just as George did when he first heard about that drive-by shooting in his hometown: with determination, love, and a remarkable tolerance for people very different than themselves. And damn if their true colors weren't just shining but changing lives—including my own.

**A few months after** my visit to TRU Colors, I heard the shocking news that Thug had been murdered. He had been staying with George's son, who helped run the brewery, while looking for a housing complex that would accept someone with a felony background. While everyone was sleeping, a gunman entered the house and killed Thug and a young woman named Briyanna. Three rival gang members were later arrested in connection with the double homicide.

Thug's murder shook TRU Colors to its core, but George and his team have doubled down on their mission. "I don't know if we'll ever get to zero," George said in a public statement after Thug's death. "Violence comes from exclusion and a lack of opportunity, and so until all of us can come together and prioritize grace and understanding over blame and divisiveness, it will never go to zero. For peace to happen, it takes the whole city uniting and committing to change."

After I sent George a short note expressing my condolences, he wrote back: "Thug was an amazing and complicated guy who had a lot of responsibility and a lot of enemies from the past. His past is what set him up for all the good he did. He's still leading, even after he's gone."

# Devote: What's in Your Suitcase?

I've been blessed to meet thousands of virtuous people in my life, people who devote themselves to the service of others. You will go on to meet many of them in this book. But I have met only one person deserving of sainthood. That's my aunt Loralee, better known to the world as Sister Loreen Spaulding.

I've spent my entire adult life learning how to put other people first, and I've made a career out of helping folks do the same. But my aunt Loralee remains the only person I've ever known who lived purely and unconditionally in service to others. There are people alive today who quite literally owe their lives to her, and I truly believe that if the rest of us could possess even a fraction of her heart, the world would be an infinitely better place. She is the embodiment of the final, and in many ways the most important, quality of influence: devotion.

Mahatma Gandhi once said that "the best way to find yourself is to lose yourself in the service of others." My aunt knew exactly who she was and what her purpose was from the day she was born. Each day, I try to honor Sister Loreen's legacy by trying to be just a little kinder and a little more patient with the people in my life, especially when it's hard. As you read her story, I ask you to do the same. And I challenge you to think about what cause you would devote yourself to if you had the time. What people in your life would you spend more time with? Which of them would you try to be better to? Most important, what is holding you back?

**When I was eight** years old, my aunt Loralee spent the night at my house in Suffern, New York, before flying the next morning to Liberia to begin an eight-year mission with the Catholic Church. When she pulled up in the cab, my mom told me to bring in her suitcase. I'd never seen one so big; the darn thing weighed more than me.

When I finally dragged it into the house, I said: "Aunt Loralee, you have so many clothes."

My aunt smiled and gestured to what she was wearing. "These are the only clothes I own, Tommy." Then she opened the massive suitcase, giving way to an avalanche of pencils and pens and kids' clothing and candy and medical supplies. All she owned was that suitcase and quite literally the clothes on her back. Then I noticed that my aunt had cut her hair. It had once been long, flowing, and beautiful.

"I donated it to a charity that helps cancer patients," she said cheerfully. "I won't need it where I'm going."

When my father was five years old, he got an electric train for Christmas; Loralee got an altar built by her grandfather. She pretended to be a priest and deliver Mass to the family, and ever since, she had been determined to become a Catholic nun. Very few people knew that, however. In school, Loralee was the all-American girl. She was a cheerleader, had lots of boyfriends, and finished as valedictorian of her class. Everyone expected her to become a scientist or a United States senator one day.

Loralee, however, had long since decided that she would

join the convent. Her dream wasn't just to live a life in the service of God but to truly make a difference in the world.

In August 1957, she kissed her boyfriend for the final time and joined the convent. She was eighteen years old. She enrolled at Notre Dame College in Euclid, Ohio, where she graduated summa cum laude with a degree in philosophy. Next up was Boston College, where she earned a master's degree in mathematics. It was about ten years later that she showed up at my house in Suffern, ready for her mission work in West Africa.

The late 1970s were a tumultuous time in Liberia. For generations, the country had been ruled by the True Whig Party, which had monopolized power and effectively banned all opposition. The country's president, William Tolbert, had promised reforms when he was elected in 1971, but his administration quickly became defined by nepotism and political corruption. My aunt Loralee, now known as Sister Loreen Spaulding, arrived in Liberia just as the country's oppressed native population began rioting in major cities. By 1977, more than a hundred Liberian citizens had been abducted, killed, and brutally dismembered in a harrowing series of murders known as the Maryland Ritual Murders (after Maryland County, Liberia).

Sister Loreen, however, was unfazed. She didn't care about Liberian politics or government corruption; she was there solely to help children. She arrived in the town of Zwedru in Liberia's southeastern region and helped build a school for young girls, many of whom were the first in their village to learn to read and write.

In early 1980, Sister Loreen traveled to Liberia's capital, Monrovia, to pick up supplies. As she was leaving a market, she heard gunshots. *Pop, pop, pop.* She ran down the street and watched as a firing squad unloaded on a dozen limp bodies lashed to trees near the beach. She would later find out that the

victims were President Tolbert and his cabinet. They had been
assassinated by Samuel Doe, a master sergeant in the Liberian
Army who had staged a coup against the government and taken
control of the country. Sister Loreen watched in horror as other
members of Tolbert's government were summarily executed on
the beach.

When she returned to her school, she tried not to think
about the chaos enveloping the country. Her job was to care for
her children and take no part in the armed conflict. But war
found the innocent, as it always does. One day, several pickup
trucks skidded to a stop in front of Sister Loreen's school and a
dozen teenagers armed with machine guns jumped out. My
aunt knew they were part of Samuel Doe's militia, a group
known to be executing tribe members loyal to the deposed
administration—even children whose only crime was being
born in the wrong village.

The soldiers shoved Sister Loreen aside and shouted in-
structions she barely understood. They had taken dozens of her
students and lined them up against a wall. Realizing what was
about to happen, my aunt pushed past the soldiers and stood in
front of her children. She stared down the rifles that were
pointed at her and shouted, "If you are going to kill these girls,
you will have to kill me first." The teenage soldiers stared at her
incredulously and then argued in their native language. Miraculously, they lowered their weapons, climbed back into their
trucks, and left. Whether they were impressed by her boldness
or afraid of shooting a Catholic nun, my aunt never knew.

The peace would not last. Doe's government was even more
corrupt and totalitarian than his predecessor's. He shut down
newspapers and rigged elections and continued his brutal
cleansing of rival ethnic groups. Allies turned on him, and the
country once again careened into a full-fledged civil war. As

rebel factions took control of the provinces, Sister Loreen's school was shut down and turned into a refugee camp. The United Nations tasked my aunt with evacuating missionaries and Peace Corps members who were stranded in Zwedru. My aunt was terrified, but she remained steadfast in her mission. After arranging transport for the others, she was the sole remaining member of her mission. Just as soldiers closed in, she fled into the rain forest, found a canoe, paddled down the Cavalla River, and escaped to Ivory Coast, where she was rescued and sent back to the United States.

Sister Loreen had spent thirteen years in Liberia and survived two revolutions, but she would not have time to rest. Shortly after Loreen returned, her mother, Auleen—my grandmother—suffered a massive stroke that left her severely incapacitated. Auleen had been a sweet, doting, and tender person, but the stroke rewired her personality into someone no one recognized. She would need round-the-clock care, so Sister Loreen spoke to the head of her order and asked permission to take a leave of absence to care for her mother. For the next thirteen years, that's what she did.

In many ways, caring for Auleen was as grueling as her missionary work in Liberia. My grandmother's stroke had left her extremely anxious, snappy, and mean. As any caregiver can attest, this sort of work takes an impossible amount of patience and fortitude. It's exhausting and thankless, and for more than a decade Sister Loreen sacrificed her well-being to keep my grandmother comfortable. When my grandmother finally died, the convent assigned Sister Loreen to be a caregiver for nuns in hospice care—a task she also performed devotedly and without complaint.

My aunt was in declining health when she turned seventy-seven, but she convinced her order to send her back to Liberia.

The bloody Liberian civil war had finally ended, but it had left a quarter million dead. Untold numbers of children were left orphaned and forced to fend for themselves on the streets. My aunt still had unfinished business in the country she loved so much, so she built an orphanage in Monrovia to help stitch Liberia back together. But fate had dealt Sister Loreen a cruel hand. Situated on the coast, Monrovia is mosquito-infested, and one morning Sister Loreen woke up with a terrible fever. She had malaria, and at her age the illness was devastating. She suffered heart failure and nearly died.

My aunt managed to recover and return to the United States, but the malaria had taken its toll. The heart failure triggered a swift mental decline, and she succumbed to dementia as the years passed. A few years after returning from Liberia, in the week of her eightieth birthday, her closest friends and family gathered at the School Sisters of Notre Dame in Wilton, Connecticut, to celebrate her sixtieth year as a Catholic nun. My aunt was frail and distant as I held her hand during Mass. That evening, at the celebratory dinner, I looked down at her as I began a toast. Beneath the wrinkles I saw the same kind, spirited person who had pulled up in a taxi in front of my house all those years ago and taught me what real leadership looked like.

I told them about "The Gift of the Magi," a 1905 short story by O. Henry about a young newlywed couple. They were poor and had very few possessions, but none of that mattered because their love was so great. They were celebrating their first Christmas together and they each secretly wanted to buy the other a special gift. The husband wanted to buy his bride a set of ornamental combs so she could adorn her long, beautiful hair. The wife wanted to buy her husband a chain for a pocket watch his deceased father had given him long ago. Because of their sacrificial love, the husband sold his father's watch to buy his beloved the combs, and the wife cut and sold all her hair so she could buy her devoted husband the chain.

"When they opened their gifts, they realized just how devoted they were to each other, and they learned just how invaluable their love truly was," I said. "Aunt Loralee, I'll never forget the gift you gave me when you showed up at my house in Suffern with your hair cut off and your suitcase filled with school supplies." I smiled at my aunt as I raised my glass. "That day you taught a selfish eight-year-old boy the true meaning of devotion and servant leadership. I've never stopped learning from your example."

Sometimes I think about all the young girls in Africa who are alive today because of my brave Aunt Loralee. I think about how she loved and served my grandmother for thirteen long years when no one else would. I think about how much better the world would be if there were just a few more Sister Loreen Spauldings out there.

# PART II

# The First *I* of Influence: Interest

# $500,000 Footlong

In the previous chapters, we looked at four amazing individuals who embody what it means to be a genuine influencer: to Lift, Embrace, Act, and Devote oneself to the service of others. But you don't have to be a teacher, a hockey prodigy, a CEO, or a Catholic nun to live a life of influence. You can **LEAD** others in big and small ways in your everyday life by learning new habits that over time become second nature. I like to call them "the three *i*'s of influence." The first is *interest,* and I can't think of a better way to explain it than by telling you about the time my friend Bill saved my butt. I had just published my first book, and I was giving a talk at the Ritz-Carlton in Palm Beach, Florida. Afterward, during the book signing, a middle-aged gentleman walked up to me.

"Hi, my name is Bill Reichel, and I just wanted to say how much I enjoyed your speech. You could have heard a pin drop in that room."

Normally I'd thank him and shake his hand and move on to the next person in line, but something about Bill piqued my curiosity. He was dressed stylishly in an Armani suit, open-collar shirt, silver chain, and leather bracelets that gave him a cool edge. Now, if you've seen me around, you'll know that I'm not the most fashionable guy out there. My idea of avant-garde is untucking my polo shirt from my GAP khaki shorts. Bill, on the other hand, looked as though he had just arrived back from New York Fashion Week.

"Let me ask you a question," I blurted. "My wife calls me the Eddie Bauer Boy. The only piece of jewelry I own is my wedding band. Jill would love me to dress a little more edgy. How can I get some cool jewelry like yours?"

Bill laughed and said, "Give me your card and I'll hook you up." True to his word, Bill mailed me a bunch of bracelets. I can't say they made me look like Johnny Depp, but they certainly upped my game. That was the beginning of our friendship.

I learned that Bill was a very successful real estate developer who owned or managed hundreds of commercial properties in the Palm Beach area. He later flew me down to speak to his employees at their annual corporate retreat, and I became close with his lovely family. His daughter, Morgan, attended our Global Youth Leadership Academy, the summer program I run for high school students, and his son, Grant, attended one of our Heart-Led Leader retreats. Bill even paid to send several inner city kids from Florida to attend the National Leadership Academy.

And when I found myself backed up against a cliff in the worst financial situation of my life, I called Bill.

As I mentioned at the beginning of this book, I had made the fateful decision to diversify my income by jumping into the sub sandwich business. I had the privilege of meeting the founder and CEO of a national sub sandwich chain and fell in love with him and his leadership team; they're as real, authentic, and genuine as they come. I was so impressed with their organization's culture and philanthropy that I went ahead and purchased a sandwich franchise in Denver.

I had high hopes for that sandwich shop. I wanted to hire local high school students and teach them the value of servant leadership. We called all our customers "ma'am" and "sir," and we said "It was an honor to serve you" as they left. I wanted that franchise to be the manifestation of every leadership lesson I had written about in my first two books. But that dream quickly became a nightmare. At our grand opening, a customer faked a fall outside our store, called an ambulance, and threatened to sue. We later found out she was a con artist who had tried this scheme numerous times. Next, we had a sewer venting problem that made the place smell like a truck stop bathroom. Worst of all, our location was terrible. Week after week, we ranked dead last among franchises in the Denver metro area. Before long I was hemorrhaging money to the tune of $10,000 per month. Within two years I had sunk more than half a million dollars into that store.

I begged my landlord to let me out of my ten-year lease. He refused. I begged the sub chain to buy me out. They refused. I was steadily going broke, and there was nothing I could do.

With no other options, I called my friend Bill.

"Bill, I'm in serious trouble," I said, tears streaming down my face. "I don't know what to do."

Most people would say, "Gee, man, that's awful. I'm sending thoughts and prayers. Let me know if I can do anything." But Bill said something I'll never forget: "Tommy, you've changed my company, you've changed my daughter's life, you've changed my son's life, you've changed my life. And now I'm going to change your life. Give me the name and number of the franchise's chief operating officer and I'll take it from there."

I've never had someone go to bat for me like that. Over the next few months, Bill had dozens of conference calls with the corporate office. He went to war with my landlord. From two thousand miles away, Bill pried open the jaws that were slowly devouring me. I'll never know exactly how he did it, but Bill got me out of that horrific situation. He never said, "Someday I'll call upon you to do a service for me," like Don Corleone in *The Godfather*. Bill just said, "Tommy, this is what friends do. They're here for each other."

When I think about how Bill saved me, I keep coming back to that simple act of curiosity that sparked our relationship. And I think about the qualities I saw in Bill, long before he came to my rescue. When I entered Bill's office for the first time, I knew within thirty seconds that he was universally beloved. You could see it in his employees' body language. Everyone was smiling. Everyone was relaxed. They told me about a time when one of their tenants, a kickboxing gym, could no longer afford their rent. Bill's response was not to boot them out but to cut their rent in half. Commercial real estate is one of the most cutthroat industries out there, and yet Bill was thriving by being a genuinely good guy. At the same time, Bill was interested in my family, my career, even my struggles. I shared everything with him, and today he knows even more about me than my therapist does. Our relationship began and flourished on a bedrock of mutual curiosity, and when I needed Bill to bail me out, he was there.

At the end of the day, Bill helped me understand that true influencers are obsessively interested in learning about the people around them, whether they're friends, co-workers, neighbors, or complete strangers. And sometimes, as we'll see, all it takes is a simple question to build a lifelong bond: What's your story?

# Everybody Has a Story

My favorite piece of artwork hangs in my office in downtown Denver. It's a beautiful watercolor of pink and blue hearts painted by a twelve-year-old. It's one of my most prized possessions, and it has a very special story.

A little over a decade ago I was speaking in Chicago to a roomful of banking executives. After my keynote I was signing copies of my book when a woman approached my table. I was immediately struck by her piercing green eyes, which seemed to gaze into my soul. She was wearing a badge that read JAYNE HLADIO. She thanked me for speaking at the event, and instead of asking her typical small-talk questions like "How are you doing today?" or "What do you do for a living?" I asked, "Hi, Jayne, what's your story?"

She looked a little caught off guard, but then she smiled, and we had a real conversation. Within five minutes I felt I had known Jayne my entire life. She has the true gift of connecting with another person. When she mentioned that she had a young daughter, Lindsey, I could tell she was just bursting with pride. "Tell me more about her," I said.

"When Lindsey was born, the doctors immediately whisked her away to surgery. She had severe multiple congenital heart defects." Jayne took a deep breath and wiped away a tear. "They told my husband and me that Lindsey had a five percent chance of survival. But she is so strong. She endured two open-heart surgeries as an infant. She survived, and today she is a totally healthy young girl."

My eyes welled up as Jayne told me this story at the book-signing table. I knew I had to meet this special girl. So the next time I was in Milwaukee, I gathered with Lindsey, Jayne, and her husband, Matt, for dinner. Ever since, we've been dear friends. It turned out that Jayne was senior vice president at U.S. Bank and one of the top business professionals in Milwaukee. You don't usually expect to find compassionate leaders in the banking industry, but Jayne is the rare exception who always puts the welfare of her employees and customers above profit. She is one of the most incredible leaders I know, and together with Lindsey she has helped raise hundreds of thousands of dollars for the American Heart Association.

In 2016, I was deeply honored when Jayne invited me to headline the annual leadership event for TEMPO, an organization composed of women who hold executive and leadership positions throughout Wisconsin. I was overwhelmed when I took the stage surrounded by more than a thousand high-powered CEOs, but my butterflies disappeared when I saw Lindsey in the crowd cheering me on. At the end of my keynote, I invited Lindsey up to the stage to congratulate her on all the money she's raised for charity. She wasn't just a future big shot—like those women in the audience, she already was one.

When my talk was over, Lindsey presented me with that lovely watercolor painting. I got teary-eyed as I hugged her and Jayne and Matt. Her artwork hangs prominently in my office to this day, and it's a reminder of the power of asking a simple question: "What's your story?"

I get it—asking people to open up is awkward. Sometimes you'll get weird looks. If you're like me, you were probably taught from an early age never to speak to strangers. That advice is right up there with "Look both ways before crossing the road." Being from New York, my parents took it a step further. "Don't look strangers in the eye," they said. "Keep your head down when you're walking." If you've ever taken the subway in New York, you know there are two important rules. The first is *Stand clear of the closing doors*. The second is *Never make eye contact*.

Think about that for a second. From childhood we are taught to ignore the people around us. It took me years to realize what terrible advice that is. When I think about the most important people in my life, it scares me to think where I would be if I hadn't spoken up when I had the chance. My wife, my best friends, nearly everyone dear to me today began as a stranger I wasn't supposed to be talking to. They would still be strangers if I hadn't bothered to find out their stories.

Here's my simple rule: Every face has a name. Every name has a story. If I introduce myself to a new person, I ask them to tell me their story. This has led to some of the most unforgettable moments of my life. For example, a few years ago, Jill and I visited Napa and Sonoma valleys with some friends. We stayed in a town called Healdsburg and did the typical wine tasting tour. On our third night we made dinner reservations at a nice restaurant in town, but first we decided to grab a drink down the road at a place called the Harmon House, which has a rooftop deck with panoramic views of the valley.

We showed up at the bar and asked the manager, Gary, for a table. "I'm so sorry, but we're fully booked," he said. "But if you'd like to catch the sunset, I'd be happy to show you the rooftop for a quick peek."

"Sure, that'd be great," we agreed.

I watched Gary as he gave us the tour, bantering with the waitstaff and schmoozing with patrons. He was doing a million different things at once yet still made us feel we were the only ones in the restaurant. Gary had the aura of a person who was purely in his element, and I was curious to know more about him.

"So, Gary, what's your story?" I asked after he finished the tour.

Gary seemed to brighten up. He smiled and told me how much he loved his job and how it made him a stronger person. He explained that he was sober, and that being near the temptation of alcohol reminded him how challenging the journey had been and how far he had come. I peppered him with more questions as Jill and our friends enjoyed the breathtaking view. Gary shared that he was recently divorced and had a young daughter. He was terrified of being the single dad who never saw his kid. Every minute he wasn't at work he made sure to spend with her. The conversation lasted only a few minutes, but I felt as if I had just heard his life story.

As we prepared to leave, Gary held up his hand. "You guys wait here for a second." He returned a minute later with four glasses of champagne. "On the house," he said. "I also managed to get you guys a table so you can enjoy the view."

Gary led us to what was clearly the best spot at the bar, a corner table overlooking the magnificent Sonoma vista. A minute later he brought out shishito peppers and other nibbles as we watched the sunset. It was the perfect way to begin our evening.

"Gary," I told him as we left, "you made this night so special. Thank you." We hugged and I asked for his card so I could send him a thank-you note. The walk to our restaurant was about ten minutes, and we did nothing but gush about Gary. *What a wonderful man. What an amazing story. I can't wait to email him.* Gary, it turns out, had one more trick up his sleeve. When we arrived at the restaurant and the hostess took us to our table, we were greeted by a chilled bottle of champagne with a note: *Thank you for the impact you had on me—Gary.* All that because I asked a guy for his story.

I share this anecdote often, and invariably someone asks me: "It just seems like you were curious about Gary to get some free stuff. How do you know if someone is being authentic or manipulative?" Admittedly, it's a fine line. When I was sixteen, I owed five dollars to the Suffern Free Library in overdue book charges. Instead of ponying up, I waltzed in and sweet-talked the librarian. I asked her questions about her life, about her favorite books, about her job—and then I asked her to waive my late fee. She did, but I felt disgusted with myself afterward. I didn't care about that librarian; I just cared about saving a few bucks. Ever since then, I have a simple rule: Be curious about other people, but never ask for anything in return. Beautiful things can happen when you form a genuine bond with someone, but your endgame should never be self-serving.

When I consult with leaders of organizations, I teach the critical importance of learning the story of each and every employee. No one embodies this philosophy better than Anthony and April Lambatos. They own and operate a catering company in Denver called Footers. I adore these two—not just because they both are genuinely good people, but because of the inclusive culture they have created at Footers. They didn't just want to build a successful company; they wanted to create a vibrant family where employees arrived in the morning pumped up to be their absolute best.

Footers's philosophy is to hire the individual, not the résumé. During interviews, they ask about stories instead of experience. They ask about hobbies and passions. They hire to improve their company's culture as well as its bottom line. Sometimes this means getting a little creative. For instance, after hiring a woman named Kari, they realized that she was not a good match for her job. While most companies would show Kari the door, that's not the philosophy at Footers. Instead, Anthony and April said: "Kari, let's find you a role here that you'll kick ass at." It took three attempts, but Kari finally found a position she could thrive in as a venue relationship manager.

Organizations like Footers are constantly learning about their employees and encouraging them to be their true selves in the workplace, however wacky. For instance, Anthony learned that one of his caterers, Lewis, had a particularly unusual story: He loved dressing in drag. Now, most employers would probably tell Lewis to do it on his own time, preferably miles from the office. Not Footers. Anthony and April arranged a company-wide lip sync battle featuring none other than Lewis as DJ, dressed in a dazzling outfit that would make RuPaul proud. Some may find Anthony and April's management style a bit abnormal, yet Footers has become one of the fastest-growing companies in Colorado, year after year winning a spot on the "Best Places to Work" list.

I've learned three things about curiosity over the years: (1) Everyone has a story, (2) people are willing to share their story if asked in an authentic way, and (3) to have a positive influence on the lives of others, we need to take the time to learn about them.

Making a habit of asking people questions about themselves sounds simple, but our brains aren't wired that way. In a

study conducted at Harvard University's Social Cognitive and
Affective Neuroscience Lab, researchers used fMRI machines
to scan participants as they discussed their own opinions and
personality traits, followed by their observations of others.
Sure enough, the "reward" areas of the brain—which are typi-
cally associated with pleasurable activities—lit up when the
participants talked about themselves. A 2017 study published
in the *Journal of Personality and Social Psychology* confirmed
that "most people spend the majority of their conversations
sharing their own views rather than focusing on the other person."

Another set of Harvard University studies scrutinized conversations during in-person speed dates. The researchers asked
some of the participants to ask as many questions as possible,
while others were instructed to ask as few as possible. Sure
enough, the study concluded, "People were more willing to go
on a second date with partners who asked more questions."

To put it another way, when you listen and ask follow-up
questions, you are telegraphing to others that you are interested in them. That kind of curiosity is the bedrock of influence,
and it's also how lifelong relationships are formed. It's how I
got to know one of my best friends, Andy Newland.

When you think "best friend," you probably think about
that pal you met in elementary school who never left your side.
Actually, I met Andy after I turned fifty. At the time, like most
guys my age, I wasn't looking to add more commitments in my
life. I was busy with three kids and a job that had me traveling
to a couple hundred cities per year. "Didn't you literally write
the book on relationships?" Jill said one day. "Yet you don't
want to meet the parents at our kids' new school."

"I'm too tired," I'd reply. "I'm too busy." You've probably

said something similar. You have your routine, and you stick to it. "I've got Corey Turer," I said. That's my best friend from way back in middle school. "I don't need another best friend."

But my daughter, Caroline, insisted that I meet her basketball coach at All Souls Catholic. "You have to meet Coach Andy," she said. "He's the best. You'll love him."

"Maybe, honey," I demurred.

"Daddy, you *have* to."

Caroline had that look on her face—the one that says *I am going to get my way no matter how long it takes*. "Fine, we'll get lunch," I groaned.

I called Andy to introduce myself, and a week later we sat down for lunch at my favorite Thai restaurant. The moment I shook his hand, I understood what Caroline saw in him. He had an aw-shucks grin and a soothing energy about him, as if his soul had been wandering the earth for thousands of years. He was missing the top of his right ear—an old wrestling injury, I assumed. At the surface level, Andy had a straightforward story that anyone could google: a kind and humble man, a committed Catholic, the president of his family-owned HVAC manufacturing and distribution company, a father of six, who volunteered his time coaching girls' basketball. Now, here's the part of his story I wouldn't have seen without asking: Andy should be dead.

After years of struggling to have children, he and his wife, Lori, were blessed with a daughter and a son after being told by doctors it would be impossible. With his life finally on track, Andy didn't want to think about the itchy mole on his ear. Finally Lori persuaded him to see a dermatologist. The diagnosis was swift: advanced melanoma. The doctor was able to remove the mole, but he warned that the cancer would likely return one day.

For seven years Andy lived his best life. He and Lori had three more kids. His HVAC company flourished. The Newlands had just closed on their dream house when Andy received the call he had been dreading. It was his oncologist—there was a spot on his lung scan. Within months, the cancer had hopscotched from organ to organ before settling in his hip lymph nodes. Andy lost fifty pounds during immunotherapy and by the end could barely get out of bed. Eventually his doctors ceased treatment and sent him home to get his affairs in order and spend his final days with his family. Lori, however, had other plans. She found a clinic in Mexico specializing in Andy's cancer and helped him summon the strength to make the trek across the border. I'm not sure what those doctors injected him with, but after convalescing in Cancún for a month and making some serious lifestyle changes, Andy was cancer-free.

Since then, Andy has learned to enjoy every sandwich. He cherishes each second with his family. Every day is a beautiful day because he is still alive, and he radiates this positivity to everyone he meets. He taught Caroline and her teammates to treasure their minutes together on the court, just as he teaches me to live every day as though I'm on borrowed time. We have dinner constantly, ride our bikes, attend Mass together. I invested my heart in that relationship because I knew that Andy would change my life, that his gentle and positive demeanor would be a vital influence when I was not appreciating life.

Every time I talk with Andy, he helps me put my problems in context and thank God for blessing me with a beautiful, healthy family. Andy is by far the greatest human being I've ever been blessed to know. I couldn't imagine what my life would be like if Caroline hadn't pushed me to have lunch with

Coach Andy, if I hadn't bothered to look him in the eye and ask, "So, what's your story?"

Who are the people in your life with faces and names but no stories attached to them? What wonderful stories could they share if only someone cared enough to ask? What new best friend is out there that you're too busy to meet?

# Turn Transactions
# into Interactions

I've lived in Colorado for over twenty years, but I'm a New Yorker at heart. And one of the things I love most about New York is the bagels. Maybe it's the city water, maybe it's the way they're boiled, maybe it's just that New York attitude, but bagels taste like cardboard anywhere else. Whenever I visit New York City, the first thing I do is grab a sesame bagel with lox and cream cheese at my favorite shop, Ess-a-Bagel on Third Avenue at Fifty-first Street. It's a family-owned, old-school New York institution. Everyone is in a hurry there, so the place is set up to move you through like a car assembly line. You order, you pay, you get your bagel, next customer.

One of the employees is a woman who has been working there for years. She is straight out of central casting, the epitome of the tough, no-nonsense New Yorker. If you don't know what you're ordering when you reach her, if you hesitate or change your mind, she'll roll her eyes and shout, "Next!" and you are unceremoniously shuttled to the back of the line. She reminds me of the Soup Nazi from *Seinfeld*, who famously screamed "No soup for you!" when a customer couldn't state their order correctly or had the gall to ask for crackers.

One day I was with my dear friend Walt Rakowich, a quintessential Colorado guy used to a friendly, laid-back style. I brought him to Ess-a-Bagel, and as we stood in line he went back and forth over what to order. *Oh man,* I thought, *the Bagel Nazi is going to eat my friend alive.* I decided to do something different this time: I would try to build a connection with her and see what happened. Why did this have to be a negative experience when it could be a positive one?

When Walt and I reached the Bagel Nazi, I worked up the courage and said, "Good morning, how are you doing today?"

She stared at me like I had given her the middle finger. "*What do you want?*" she demanded.

"I come here every time I visit the city. I just wanted to introduce myself. I'm Tommy, and I think you make the best bagels in the world. This is my friend Walt. What's your name?"

I braced for the worst, but something about her expression seemed to crack. "Barbara," she answered skeptically, as if trying to calculate my motive. But I sensed the tiniest bit of warmth. At that moment she seemed to transform before my eyes. She wasn't this cold New Yorker; she was another human being with her own life and her own set of problems, just like Walt and me. She wasn't the Bagel Nazi. She was Barbara.

As we ordered our bagels, we started asking her questions. *How long have you been working here? What's your favorite bagel?* I asked about her family. With every question her face brightened. We were interested in her life. We had moved from a transactional relationship to something deeper.

At one point she asked, "Hey, do you guys want some water? We usually have complimentary plastic cups, but we're all out right now. Tell you what—" She walked over to the fridge and grabbed us two bottled waters. And then she did something I'll never forget: She opened her purse and added three dollars to the register. "On me," she said with a big smile.

I was so touched. "Barbara," I said, "thank you so much. You have made my day. Do you mind if I give you a hug?"

"I would *love* one," she replied, her voice cracking as if she had been waiting for a hug all her life. She came around the register and wrapped me in a bear hug. "Bless you," she said.

"Barbara," I told her, "I'm going to come back with my family the next time we visit the city and I'm always going to ask for you."

After we walked away, Barbara reverted to her typical New York swagger. "*What do you want? Next!*" But there was just a tiny bit more warmth in her voice, a tiny bit more patience. There was no way she woke up that morning thinking she would hug a customer, but Walt and I had changed the direction of her day simply by treating her like a human being. I don't know how far that influence ripple will go, but I know I felt good about myself for days after, and I like to think Barbara did too.

Our lives are filled with Barbaras—people we regularly transact with but don't interact with. We don't just have this problem in line for bagels and coffee, however. A recent Harris poll found that while many managers struggle to deliver negative feedback to their direct reports—no surprise there, as any boss can attest—an astounding 69 percent admit that "communicating in general" is the hardest part about dealing with their employees. Yes, you read that right: *communicating in general*. In other words, acting like a normal human being. Why is it so hard to develop meaningful relationships with people we transact with?

Even I struggled with this for years until I learned a simple technique: Make someone's day. All it involves is finding someone you'd normally transact with—whether it's a cashier, a barista, or Bob from accounting—and make their day unforgettable with a simple gesture. Be curious and ask questions about their life, then identify one way you can make them smile. It's that simple.

Here's an example. Since I'm on the road a couple hundred days per year, my clothes are often in rough shape. I stuff trousers into carry-on bags, throw suit jackets over my shoulder as I'm running to catch a flight, spill coffee on everything. On top of that, my weight goes up and down like a yo-yo, so I need a quality tailor. For years I've relied on a woman named Hilda Mayr, who operates out of a tiny shop in Denver. Hilda grew up in Germany before immigrating to the United States in the 1960s. She hasn't forgotten any of that German efficiency, nor does she suffer fools lightly. Or make chitchat. Or really any conversation that doesn't have to do with her work. When I walk into her tailor shop to have my trousers hemmed, Hilda says, "Hello. Okay. Put on your pants."

No matter how much I tried to get to know her, Hilda was resistant to my overtures. In her defense, Hilda doesn't have much time to talk. In her "spare time" she does all the uniform repairs, alterations, and name badges for the Denver Broncos. The team entrusted Hilda to sew the Super Bowl patches for their 2016 championship. She even stays up during draft night to sew name badges for incoming players meeting the press the following morning. That might be a full-time job for anyone else, but Hilda and her husband also run a dry cleaning service for klutzes like me who leave a river of spilled coffee in their wake.

A while back I walked into Hilda's shop because I needed a new suit. The appointment started off as usual: "Hold out your arm. Now the other arm. Turn around." And so on. It pained me that I saw this woman so often and yet I knew nothing about her.

"Hilda," I asked one day, "what's your favorite food?"

Hilda gave me a severe look, then muttered: "Hamburger with American cheese." Well, when I walked into Hilda's shop a week later to pick up my suit, I brought her a big, juicy burger with American cheese. She looked at me for a moment, stunned, and then broke into a big smile. Ever since, it has been our little ritual. When I go to see Hilda, I bring her a cheeseburger.

It was my simple interactions with Hilda that helped me get through the COVID-19 pandemic. I love seeing people, hugging them, and simply being close, and I couldn't do much of that for most of 2020. A week before Christmas, I walked into her shop to get my pants hemmed. We said our hellos through our masks, but instead of a cheeseburger, I handed her a bottle of wine and a handwritten card.

"Merry Christmas, Hilda!" I said.

When I handed Hilda her gift, all that German toughness evaporated. Her eyes welled up, then she said softly: "I've been working here for forty years. I've had thousands and thousands of customers, Tommy, and none of them have ever brought me a Christmas gift. I am so thankful for you." I don't count Hilda among my closest friends, but that moment made us both cry. After months of not being able to be near people, Hilda's words reassured me that everything would be okay. A moment of warmth after so much cold. We're all in this together.

Go ahead and make a list of all the people you interact with in your day-to-day routine. This might sound daunting until you realize just how small our bubbles are, how few people we truly have meaningful conversations with. Make it a goal—maybe once per week—to identify a person you *see* but don't *know,* and then make them smile.

Here's another fun one to try: Make a total stranger's day. About seven years ago I was in the Ozarks at the Missouri As-

sociation of Secondary Education Principals. I was invited by
my friend Jennifer Strauser, an associate high school principal
in Eureka, Missouri. She is one of the finest educators I've ever
met. Jennifer has repeatedly turned down the top job at her
school because it would mean having to spend more time behind a desk and less time working with kids.

This conference was teenage me's worst nightmare: being
stuck in a room with seven hundred school principals. They
weren't there to give me detention, fortunately; I was giving the
keynote address. That's right, for once, *I* was giving the lecture!
After the conference, Jennifer suggested we grab a bite to eat on
the way to the airport, so we stopped off at a little hole-in-the-
wall diner. Now, you haven't seen rural until you've seen the
Ozarks. Sprawling riverways, rolling hills, lush pasture—you
can drive for miles without seeing another person. This little
diner was nearly empty, and a bit run-down, and the waitress
almost looked surprised to see us walk in the door. She handed
us laminated menus and then poured coffee that tasted as if it
had been in the pot for a few days. Needless to say, I had low
expectations as I ordered my omelet.

When I sliced it open and took a bite, I dropped my fork. It
was the best omelet I had ever tasted. The eggs, the cheese, the
sausage, the mushrooms, the scallions, the diced avocados—
they all melted together into pure perfection. *Heaven isn't in
the sky,* I thought, *it's in the kitchen of this diner in the Ozarks.*
I was overcome with the need to *do something*. I couldn't just
eat this perfect omelet, leave a few crumpled bills, and leave.

"I think I have to meet the chef!" I said to Jennifer.

"For an omelet? Only you, Tommy," she laughed.

I immediately called the waitress over. "Excuse me, I need to
speak with the chef. This is the best omelet I've ever had in my
life."

The waitress looked slightly confused but agreed to pass on my message. A few minutes later the chef walked out. He was a gangly kid in his early twenties wearing a backward baseball cap. I asked him his name. "Mike," he said. I introduced myself and invited him to sit down, then looked him square in the eye and told him what a delicious meal he had cooked. I told him that I'd been to five-star restaurants in New York and L.A., I'd eaten food prepared by celebrity chefs trained in the finest culinary institutes—none of those dishes compared to the omelet this aw-shucks kid from Missouri had whipped up in five minutes. I told Mike that if I came back to the Ozarks in ten years and he hadn't opened his own restaurant by then, I'd kick his ass. We shook hands, and Mike left our table grinning from ear to ear.

Fast-forward five years, and Jennifer was attending the graduation ceremony for our annual National Leadership Academy in Denver. Her school district sends thirty students every year to the NLA, and she takes time from her well-deserved summer vacation each year to cheer them on as they graduate. This ceremony was especially important as it was the twentieth anniversary of the NLA's founding, and we could all reflect on how far we'd come. As I prepared to step onstage to give my closing remarks, I overheard Jennifer chatting with a friend of hers, who was attending for the first time.

"Tell me about this guy Tommy Spaulding," the friend said.

I expected Jennifer to tell her about my time with Up with People, or about my books, or about my work with business leaders. Blah, blah, blah. The kind of bullet-points stuff you put on your LinkedIn profile. Instead, Jennifer said: "Let me tell you about the time Tommy and I walked into a diner in the Ozarks . . ." Jennifer didn't care about my credentials or my awards. She cared about a moment of influence that left a last-

ing impression not only on Mike the omelet chef but on Jennifer herself.

I don't know if Mike will own his own restaurant one day—
maybe his hopes and dreams lie elsewhere—but I like to think
he will always cherish that time a random customer came into
his diner and told him he made one hell of an omelet. And I like
to think that Mike will be one of the eighty thousand people
cheering in my stadium one day.

Imagine walking down the street knowing that at any moment, you could dramatically influence the life of a complete
stranger. Everyone has this power, if only we choose to use it.

Here's a great way to start small: Give a stranger a compliment.

Charlotte Haigh was walking down a London street one
day when a woman caught her eye. She was wearing a gorgeous red dress, and Charlotte had the urge to tell her how
great she looked. But shyness got the better of her. Later, Charlotte felt ashamed for not speaking up. "After all, there's enough
meanness and criticism in the world," she explained in *Prima*
magazine. The next day, when she was followed out of a store
by a woman wearing a chic white shirt and flared jeans, she
decided to go for it.

"You look amazing," she said bluntly.

The woman stopped short and smiled, and then her eyes
filled with tears. "You don't know what a lift that's given me,"
she replied. "I'm going through a divorce now and I'm having
a terrible day. You really cheered me up."

From then on, Charlotte made it a daily practice to give
compliments to strangers. Whether it's someone's stunning blue
eyes, their freckles, or their fashion choices, her only rule is to
be sincere. She is occasionally met with embarrassed glances,

but most of the time her compliments lead to warm exchanges and genuine gratitude.

About a week in, Charlotte realized that her experiment was making her feel a lot better about herself. "I'm hoping my compliments create a ripple effect," she wrote. "Just yesterday, a woman approached me in a department store to tell me how stylish I looked. I wonder whether she did that because a stranger once said something lovely about her—I like to think of it as compliment karma."

Making someone's day unforgettable, whether it's through a heartfelt gesture or a perfectly delivered compliment, isn't just a nice thing to do; you are deeply and positively affecting that person's brain chemistry. One study found that compliments and praise help people learn new motor skills and behaviors. Moreover, receiving kind words activates the ventral striatum, better known as the brain's reward center. In fact, one team of researchers using MRI machines discovered that receiving a compliment is just as thrilling to the brain as finding a big wad of cash. I guess there really is something to that old expression "You look like a million bucks!"

# Make Kindness Normal

One of the most talented public speakers I know is a young man named Houston Kraft. Houston is an author, curriculum designer, and kindness advocate who speaks at schools, conferences, and youth events internationally. He's only in his early thirties, but Houston has spoken to half a million young people at six hundred events, including delivering the 2017 keynote address at our National Leadership Academy. His organization, CharacterStrong, builds curricula that foster compassionate culture in twenty-five hundred schools serving more than a million kids. That's the long version of his bio. Here's the short version: Houston Kraft is the nicest guy I've ever met.

There's a story Houston tells often that gets to a second, more uncomfortable way we can become more interested in others. It's one thing to be curious about another person's hobbies or interests. It's another thing entirely to be curious about why a person is in pain and how you can make it better. Except that is precisely what Houston does. Some years ago, he boarded a plane for home after completing a whirlwind tour of speaking engagements. He was exhausted, and just as Houston was ready to collapse into his seat and take a nap, the woman next to him tapped him on the shoulder.

"Hi! My name is Helga!"

Being the nicest guy in the world, Houston sat up and introduced himself. They got to talking about an organization he started in high school called RAKE (Random Acts of Kindness, Etc.). Suddenly Helga grew somber.

"There's nothing more important in the world than kindness," she said, then went quiet. Most people would nod and take advantage of the pause to end the conversation and get some sleep. But Houston was curious. This was clearly a sore spot for Helga.

"Why do you say that?" he asked gently.

Helga took a deep breath and told Houston about the last time she had been on a plane. It was three years ago, and she was flying to Washington, D.C., because her dad's health had taken a turn for the worse. During her flight she was thinking about all the things she wanted to say to her father. All the memories she wanted to thank him for. The words she would use to say her final goodbye. But when the plane landed, her sister called: Her father had just passed away. Helga sat on the plane in stunned silence, dimly aware of her fellow passengers chatting and gathering their belongings. When Helga deplaned in Dulles International Airport, she crumpled into a ball along the nearest wall and began to cry uncontrollably. She wailed and moaned and sobbed as the realization set in: She would never get to see the most important person in her life ever again. And she never even got to say goodbye.

Here's the part that made Houston himself cry, and it's the reason he tells this story in all his speeches. "Houston," Helga said, "not a single person stopped and asked if I was okay. Not one person asked how they could help. Not one person put their hand on my shoulder and said, 'Is there anything I can do?' Not one person. It was that day I realized how much we need each other. It was that day I realized that kindness isn't normal."

*Kindness isn't normal.* Is that what we've become? The hundreds of people who walked by as Helga bawled her eyes out probably wouldn't consider themselves unkind. They have families and jobs, and they do good things every single day for the people they love. But a stranger crying alone in the airport? We look away and keep walking. Ever since that experience, Houston has been on the lookout for Helgas—"for the little opportunities that surround me every day to practice making kindness my default setting," he says.

When I heard Houston's story, I thought back to a girl I knew in middle school named Kathleen. Our families went to Sacred Heart Catholic Church in Suffern, New York, together. They were one of the kindest families you'll ever meet, and Kathleen was no exception. She always had a smile on her face. And she had the warmest blue eyes. Unfortunately, Kathleen suffered from psoriasis, and her skin looked as if she'd been severely sunburned. Some of our classmates teased her. They called her "scabby" and "peeled tomato." I never joined in, but I also never raised a finger to shut them up. That duty went to Kathleen's brother, Rich, who made sure that anyone who made fun of his little sister went home with a black eye.

One day, I was sitting next to Kathleen at Mass when it was time for the congregation to join hands and pray together. Kathleen didn't move her arm; she expected me to avoid touching her, like everyone else. But I was suddenly curious to see what all the fuss was about. Was Kathleen really all that different than me? So what if she had itchy skin? I took Kathleen's hand and held it tight, and she smiled at me. That was the beginning of our friendship.

Houston's story also made me think about Chad Harris, a guy I met my freshman year of college. We lived in the same residence hall at East Carolina University—he was in 142 Garrett Hall, and I was in 120. Like Kathleen, Chad was someone people tended to avoid. One year earlier, Chad had dived head-first into shallow water and hit his head on some rocks. He broke his neck and became paralyzed from the neck down. Suddenly Chad became one of those people you make sure to smile at and hold the door open for but never really get to know.

One day I ran into Chad's stepfather, Ray, in Garrett Hall. He and his wife were staying in a nearby hotel caring for Chad while he lived on campus. Out of the blue, Ray asked me if I wanted a part-time job caring for Chad. He couldn't pay more than minimum wage—only a few bucks per hour back then. I could make more money in a weekend bartending than I could in a month caring for Chad, but money was money, and I was a broke college kid.

"I would love to," I said.

But something amazing happened. I fell in love with Chad's heart and his devilish sense of humor. He was the world's biggest Grateful Dead fan and became famous around campus for his tie-dyed shirts. Chad could defuse any uncomfortable situation with the perfect joke—his favorite was "Don't make me get out of this chair and kick your ass!" But most of all, I was inspired by his unrelenting positivity.

Before long, I cared for Chad not because I was paid to, but because I loved him like a brother. Every day I fed him. I helped him shower, go to the bathroom, get dressed, and get ready for class. I became acutely aware of just how inaccessible public spaces are. I got angry when I saw steps going into a building, but no ramps. Discrimination spoken with bricks and concrete instead of words. Chad once told me it made him angry seeing able-bodied students slap the accessibility button to swing open the library door because they were too lazy to open it themselves. People have no idea how fortunate they are simply to be walking around, and to this day I cringe when people undeservingly use that button. Thanks to Chad, I saw the world through an entirely new lens.

During junior and senior years, Chad and I went on spring break together to Florida. We saw the Grateful Dead in concert. After graduation, we bought Eurail Passes and backpacked across Europe. We went to the top of the Eiffel Tower and toured the Colosseum. I no longer saw the wheelchair or a man paralyzed from the neck down. Instead, I saw a guy with instant wit and a beautiful heart. A guy who helped me when I was struggling with dyslexia and failing most of my college classes. When I felt angry at God for making it so difficult for me to read, I thought about how that shallow water had robbed Chad of a lifetime of mobility. That didn't stop him from loving life, and I knew I couldn't let a bunch of scrambled words on a page stop me from loving mine.

I know Chad didn't need me to live life to the fullest—and in the end, he was a far bigger influence on me than I was on him—but one of the greatest joys of my life was working as his caregiver for those four years and learning how to make kindness just a bit more normal.

Before we wrap up this chapter, I want you to imagine for a moment what happens when an entire organization is filled with people who are on a mission to make kindness normal. I've been fortunate enough to see a lot of them in my life, but one of my favorite examples is from an Italian restaurant in

Toronto called Trattoria Nervosa. The hundred-seat establishment occupies an old Victorian house surrounded by modern high-rises, like a glimpse of the old country in the big city. It's a familycentric spot with an old-school Italian vibe. About six years ago I was in town with my son Tate, who was then eight years old, for a hockey tournament. One night we stumbled onto Trattoria Nervosa, hoping for something simple and familiar since Tate was under the weather.

The place was packed on a Sunday night. After waiting forty-five minutes, we got a small table upstairs, and our waitress immediately noticed that Tate wasn't feeling well. She was a mom herself, she explained, and a mom can always tell when a little boy or girl is sick.

"Have you given him any Motrin?" she asked me.

"No," I replied, a little embarrassed. I wasn't even sure what Motrin was.

The waitress smiled warmly and said, "No problem. I'll run over to the pharmacy across the street and get him some." I was speechless—the restaurant was packed to the gills, and yet our waitress was kind enough to run to the pharmacy. Who does that? She returned in a few minutes and apologized because the pharmacy was closed. I began to thank her for trying, but she cut me off. "Don't worry, my manager is going to take care of it."

A minute later a well-built guy in a button-down shirt approached our table and said in a thick Italian accent, "We found a late-night pharmacy ten minutes away, and one of our busboys is in a cab right now getting your Motrin. My name is Christian Alfarone, and please let me know if I can do anything else for you."

*They sent a busboy in a cab?* I thought. *Who does that?*

I glanced down at my plate and bit my lip. We weren't some group of big shots slinging back $500 bottles of wine. We had ordered an $18 plate of spaghetti and meatballs for the two of us. Our bill wouldn't even cover the cab fare.

Christian seemed to sense my unease. "It's no problem at all," he said. "We're just happy you visited us tonight." A half hour later a busboy arrived at our table and delivered the Motrin, and Tate's fever was gone by the time we finished dessert. When we left the restaurant, I tried to pay for the medicine and cab fare, but Christian waved me off. "It's my pleasure, sir," he said. "Please come back next time you are in Toronto." I took his card and made a point to send him a thank-you note.

When I got home, I mailed Christian a dozen copies of my second book, *The Heart-Led Leader,* for him to share with his staff. I told him that he was a genuine servant leader and that he ought to be proud of the amazing work he had done with Trattoria Nervosa. We became fast friends, and I've sent hundreds of new customers to his restaurant.

Christian is a fixture of my keynote addresses these days, all due to that bottle of Motrin. Everyone who works for his restaurant, I tell my audiences, is an ambassador of positive influence. Every single employee, from the cooks to the waitstaff to the ownership, understands how much goodwill you generate by making kindness normal. That ten-dollar bottle of Motrin wasn't just a good deed; it was an investment in a lifelong customer, and for Christian, investments like these are paying off. The revenue of his quaint little establishment is more than triple that of the average Canadian restaurant of similar size. *Triple.* And it has nothing to do with the food. Christian once explained to me that he is not in the restaurant business. "My job is not making spaghetti and meatballs. I'm in the influence business. I'm going to influence every single member of my team, and they will influence every single person who walks into my restaurant."

When you make kindness normal on a regular basis, the long-term results can be anything but routine. Here's one of my favorite stories of all time: From a very early age, my stepson, Anthony, has been fixated on serving others. When he was eighteen, he decided he wanted to do it for a living, beginning with enrolling in the United States Air Force Academy in Colorado Springs. Anthony loves structure, he loved leading his hockey team, and he loves his country, so Jill and I agreed to do everything we could to help him fulfill his dream.

Getting into the Air Force Academy isn't like applying to a typical college. In addition to elite grades, you need elite character. You need to be the very best at everything you do. And you also need a member of Congress to recommend you. Well, Anthony is certainly the best at nearly everything he does, and I don't know a more honorable young man, but his grades were not quite elite. He graduated from high school with a 3.65 GPA, and the average entering cadet had a 3.87. But he put together his application, and on a cold November day Anthony stood in line outside U.S. senator Michael Bennet's office in downtown Denver. He would be one of dozens of young people interviewing in front of a panel for one of the senator's ten Air Force Academy slots.

The interview went well, but we knew the odds were slim that he would win a nomination, due to his good but not elite GPA. Nevertheless, I wanted to tell him how proud I was of him, so Anthony and I made plans to get lunch the next day before his flight back to Canada, where he was playing junior hockey. But at the last minute, Anthony canceled. I didn't ask him why when I dropped him off at the airport later that afternoon, though I felt a little hurt. I would have loved that quality time with him.

When I brought it up with Jill later that day, she gave me a look. "You mean he didn't tell you why?" She explained that while Anthony was waiting outside in line to interview at Senator Bennet's office, he'd struck up a conversation with a homeless man. Most people stare through the homeless, as if pretending they don't exist is somehow polite. Not Anthony. He sat down with him. The man had lost his job and was just trying to turn his life around, Anthony learned. Instead of nodding along and saying, "Good luck," Anthony asked the man what he needed. The next day he canceled lunch with me so he could drive to the supermarket and purchase, with his own money, shaving cream, deodorant, socks, beef jerky, and other essentials. Then he drove downtown, found the man, and gave him the shopping bag full of supplies. Anthony never thought to tell me because it wasn't something he wanted credit for. He didn't want a pat on the back. Anthony knows that being kind isn't something you brag about, it's just something you do.

A month later I was on vacation in Maui with Caroline and Tate. I met up with a longtime friend, Adam Agron. Adam is the managing partner of one of the largest and most successful law firms in the western United States. We were chatting before dinner, and I mentioned that Anthony was applying to the Air Force Academy. When I told him what Anthony had done for the homeless man, his eyes welled up.

"Tommy," he said. "I'm going to make a phone call for Anthony."

It turns out that that phone call was to Senator Michael Bennet's office. He knew the senator and his chief of staff, and he wanted the nominating committee to know the kind of man they were considering for entrance to the academy. In the end,

Anthony did not receive a nomination to the Air Force Academy. We later heard that it was one of the most competitive years ever, and his scores were not quite there. But that's not where this story ends. In January, Anthony received a letter in the mail. It was from Senator Bennet's office. The senator had nominated Anthony for admission to the United States Military Academy at West Point—a school that grooms the five-star generals, presidents, and Fortune 500 CEOs of tomorrow.

When Anthony went off to West Point in June 2021, he took his oath of service on the famous parade field where so many of the country's best leaders had stood before him. He recited the same oath taken by Grant, MacArthur, Eisenhower, and Patton, and then he disappeared into a sea of cadets in white dress uniforms. As Anthony began the next stage of his promising young life, I thought about how that single act of influence had led him on an incredible and unexpected journey eighteen hundred miles across the country to one of the most vaunted institutions in America.

I can't guarantee that these wonderful things will happen when you are good to others, but I can promise you'll feel better about yourself. And your kindness may even rub off. A 2010 study published in *Proceedings of the National Academy of Sciences* proved that generosity is highly contagious. The researchers studied people as they played a board game that rewarded acts of greed. The nastier you were, the better you did. However, when a single player decided to be generous instead of self-serving, the dynamics of the game broke down. Instead of acting out of greed, the other players responded with similar acts of generosity. That one act created a ripple of kindness that continued to grow, even though the players were acting against their self-interest.

What are the ways you can make kindness normal in your

life? Here's a good place to start: Think of the people you instinctively look away from. The people whose circumstances make you uncomfortable. Be genuinely interested in their stories, then go one step further and be interested in how you can help. It may or may not change their lives, but it certainly will change yours.

# PART III

# The Second /
# of Influence:
# Investment

# What's My Legacy?

**M**y friends tend to groan when I bring up my mentor Jerry Middel in conversation. They nod along politely, but I know what they're thinking: *Oh great, another Jerry story.*

If you've read my first two books—or talked to me for more than five minutes—you know that I can't stop raving about Jerry. Next to my wife, kids, and parents, he's the most important person in my life. Just about every week for the past two decades we've had breakfast or a phone call together. "How's your family?" he asks. "How's business? How's Tommy? What can I do?" Jerry gave the prayer at my wedding. When Jill and I didn't have the credit to buy our first home, he co-signed our mortgage. He got me back on track with my faith. He's donated tens of thousands of dollars to the National Leadership Academy. He's been such a father figure to me that I call him Pops.

But here's a Jerry story I haven't told before. When his seventy-fifth birthday rolled around a few years ago, I wanted to do something special for him. For years, our conversations had revolved around my struggles, my successes, my life—me, me, me. For one night, I wanted it to be just about Jerry. I called his wife, Joyce, and asked if I could borrow him on his special birthday, and she agreed. We hopped in my car and drove two hours to Vail, Colorado, where I'd rented a suite. We had a fancy steak dinner and brought back a bottle of bourbon to the room. And then we talked. We talked as evening slipped into morning, with only the depleted bottle of Blanton's to mark the passage of time. We talked about our lives, about our marriages, about our children, about our fears. Jerry opened up about his time in the Vietnam War, which he almost never speaks about. And then we talked about something that I will never forget.

"Tommy, what is my legacy?" he asked with a wistfulness I had not heard before.

"What do you mean?" I replied. How could a man who had done so much good in his life not know his own legacy?

"I've made a lot of money in my life. I have a very successful business. I've mentored a handful of kids. I've donated to charities, and I've served on many of their boards. But is that my legacy? Giving money to other people who change lives?"

Jerry set down his bourbon glass and looked me in the eye. He was tearing up. "Tommy, you've personally helped tens of thousands of kids learn leadership skills. You've started a nonprofit and written two bestselling books and touched hearts around the world. People will be reading your words and listening to your speeches long after you're gone. Me? I haven't written any books or given speeches to thousands of people. I've just tried to be a good husband, father, and businessman, and to stay involved in my community. But I haven't had a big impact. I haven't changed anything."

I stared at him as he went quiet. Then I smiled and said, "Jerry, are you ready for your ass-whooping?" It was the same line Jerry always used when I hadn't been a good father, husband, or boss. For the first time ever, I threw it back at him.

I spent the next half hour putting Jerry in his place. "You're looking at this all wrong," I said. "Sure, some people start non-profits and donate buildings for the world to see. Maybe they have a great legacy, maybe they don't. But you've poured everything into our relationship. You've literally changed my life. You've had more of an influence on me than any other person on the planet. *That* is legacy. Leaving a legacy means you've made the life of another person better. I would never have started my charity and helped all those kids if you hadn't supported me every step of the way. You invested in me, and all the good I've done is as much your legacy as it is mine."

When I finished, Jerry beamed at me. He got it. I realized that this pain had been building inside him in recent years as he reached the twilight of his life. It made me proud to do right by him after being on the receiving end of his love for so long.

Over the following weeks and months, I thought about what Jerry had said to me. I thought a lot about how my mentor's legacy will ripple onward in so many strange and beautiful ways for generations to come. His influence on me can be measured in almost geological time, punctuated by our weekly breakfasts and phone calls, the regular check-ins, his encouragement during good times, and his rocklike presence during bad times. Jerry's relentless determination to stay in my life is the single greatest lesson on influence I've ever learned.

In the previous section, we saw that being interested in other people is the gateway to lasting influence. Now we're going to see what happens when you take the next step and invest for the long term in the lives of others. The next chapters are about broadening your sphere of influence. For most people, that sphere encompasses their parents, grandparents, children, and maybe a few close friends. You take care of that sphere—tend to your own garden, mow your own lawn, shovel your own driveway. But what if you could expand that legacy beyond the nuclear family, to distant friends, co-workers, and clients? To your plumber, your barber, your favorite customer? The greatest influencers—people like Jerry Middel—relentlessly expand their influence sphere and leave behind a piece of their legacy in anyone who is fortunate enough to cross their path.

It sounds like a lot of work, but it's easy. All you have to do to get started is follow a simple rule: Own your words.

# Own Your Words

Let me tell you a story about a woman named Nancy. Today, she and her husband run a church that serves tens of thousands of people. Years ago, when they were starting their church, Nancy made it a point to get to know everyone in her congregation.

One day she met a single mom named Maggie. It was obvious that Maggie was struggling to get by. Her clothes were shabby, and when Nancy drove by her house for a visit, she noticed the lawn was overgrown with weeds. The roof was missing shingles, the paint was chipped—the list went on. As she knocked on the door, Nancy made a mental note of everything that needed a little TLC. Maggie invited her in, but she was clearly embarrassed by the state of her home. The floors were dirty, no one had dusted for weeks, the windows were caked with grime. Nancy noted everything she saw. Finally she arrived at the kitchen, which was woefully understocked. Nearly all the food in the fridge was for the baby. As a single mother, it was very difficult to make enough to feed two mouths.

Nancy said goodbye and drove straight home, where she wrote down a list of everything Maggie needed: The lawn needed to be mowed and weed-whacked. The roof needed repairs. The house needed a paint job. The windows needed to be washed. The interior needed a deep clean, and all the rooms needed to be tidied. Most of all, Maggie needed her kitchen restocked with the essentials. Nancy made plans to start a food drive and get other members of the congregation to chip in to make Maggie's life just a little bit easier. After all, she thought, what good was a church if it didn't come together to help those in need?

Do you know what Nancy did next? Absolutely nothing.

Life got busy. She had a church to run and a family to raise. She had a deluge of phone calls and emails to respond to, events to plan and meetings to attend. Maggie's list got buried in a sea of grocery trips and wedding invitations and the other typical obligations of a person who never has enough time on her hands.

Nancy's story isn't unique. It happens all the time. You make a list of things to do, and then life gets in the way. You have the grandest intentions, but there's never enough time. Work gets crazy. The kids have soccer practice. Your marriage goes through a rough patch. Sometimes the things we forget to do are small, like wishing a friend a happy birthday. Sometimes they are bigger, like forgetting to visit them in the hospital during an illness.

Research overwhelmingly shows that most people regret the things they *didn't* do more than the things they did. For instance, studies of hospice patients show that, above everything else, they regret not being more loving to those who matter most. They remember all the times they missed out on the little opportunities to express their love because they had a call, they were tired, because a million unimportant things seemed more important at the time.

I'm a music lover. I love jamming to Billy Joel, Journey, and the Eagles in the car. But there's one song I love for a different reason. It's "Cat's in the Cradle" by Harry Chapin. No song has ever had more of an influence on me. It's a heartbreaking story about a father who never has enough time with his son. The boy takes his first steps while he's away on business. Then the father is too busy to have a game of catch when his boy is ten. He always works late instead of coming home. The song's recurring verse has the son saying, "I'm gonna be like you, Dad, you know I'm gonna be like you." Then, when the father is old and finally has time for his family, his son is all grown up and has a demanding job of his own and too many obligations. He doesn't have time to see his dad. "He'd grown up just like me," the father laments as the song ends. "My boy was just like me."

I cry every single time I hear that song. Whenever Tate wants to play catch or shoot the puck around, I drop what I'm doing and meet him outside. I was determined to be as good a father as mine was to me. When I got home from school each day, my father was always there. He never missed a single football game, Boy Scout event, or school musical. He never missed a family dinner. I desperately wanted Tate to be able to recall the same things about me one day.

I also think about the pastor's wife when I hear "Cat's in the Cradle." I think about all the little things we say we'll do for others, and how all those promises get crushed to dust under the weight of everyday life. You can have every intention in the world of being a positive influence on those around you. You can make plans and write down lists, but they're all for nothing unless you convert those words into action. Unless you own your words and the promises you make with them.

For me, the epitome of a place that can't do what they say is the car dealership. The salesperson promises a price when

they're showing you the car, but as soon as you reach the signing table they're tacking on destination fees, document fees,
trade-in fees, financing fees—thousands of dollars more than
you thought you were paying. When I bought my car a few
years ago, the sales manager promised he'd send me a golf
sweater that I admired him wearing. But once I signed on the
dotted line, I never heard from him. He didn't own his words.
That single experience was enough for me to swear that I'd
never buy a car from that dealership again.

I know, it's just a golf sweater. I probably would have worn
it twice. But the sales manager broke a promise, and as researchers at the London School of Economics found out, breaking promises is indeed bad for business. After observing
hundreds of employees in the medical field, the researchers
found that when an employee perceives that their employer has
broken its word—say, a promised raise, promotion, or fringe
benefit—that employee may subconsciously "exhibit negative
behaviours towards other innocent parties such as co-workers
and clients." In other words, the negative influence from a single broken promise is so toxic that we're more likely to "pay it
forward" to colleagues and clients and make the situation far
worse.

But the positive influence of keeping your promise can be
just as powerful. When I first moved to Denver in 1999, I met
a guy named Ed Larkin. He had season tickets for the Colorado
Avalanche and offered to sell me a handful of games. The prices
went up and down depending on the schedule, and Ed promised to mail me a check at the end of the season for any amount
I had overpaid. Well, the following April, an envelope arrived in
the mail from Ed. Inside was a check for $0.23—less than the
stamp had cost! Ed had given me his word to repay any amount,
and he followed through. Over two decades later, whenever I

make a promise to someone, I think about Ed and the lasting influence of his $0.23 check.

The thing about owning your words is that you don't have to go overboard. "Just keep your promises: Going above and beyond does not pay off," concluded a study by the University of California, San Diego. In a series of experiments exploring promise breaking, promise keeping, and promise exceeding, the researchers found that while people reacted very negatively when a promise was broken, the effect of greatly exceeding a promise was almost nothing. For example, if you are sending flowers to Mom on Mother's Day, you're better off with a simple bunch of roses that arrives on time than an over-the-top bouquet that arrives late. "When you keep a promise, not only have you done something nice for someone, but you've also fulfilled a social contract and shown that you're a reliable and trustworthy person," the researchers explained. "Invest efforts into keeping promises, not in exceeding them."

The greatest influencers I know are always investing their efforts in keeping their promises. For example, when my dear friend Frank DeAngelis makes a promise to someone, he makes it for life. He was principal of Columbine High School when two students stalked the hallways with assault weapons and perpetrated what was then the deadliest school shooting in U.S. history. In the aftermath of the massacre, Frank pledged to help the surviving students rebuild and forge a new identity for the school, delaying his retirement until students who had been kindergarteners at the time of the massacre graduated from Columbine High School. I was fortunate enough to attend Frank's retirement ceremony after that final class had graduated. Hundreds of people were there, each of them clutching a stack of handwritten letters from Frank over the years. Christmas cards, birthday cards, thank-you cards, sympathy cards—

everyone from parents to students to secretaries to coaches had a story about how Frank had touched their lives.

But Frank follows through on his pledges even when the eyes of the world move on. About seven years ago, Frank and I were at our National Leadership Academy's annual Book-n-Benefit business breakfast, of which Frank serves as honorary chairman. The keynote speaker, the renowned educator and business coach Dr. Marshall Goldsmith, challenged his audience to make a commitment to serve something or someone beyond themselves—and to remain dedicated to that promise for the rest of their lives. I committed to praying the rosary every morning. Frank turned to me and said, "Tommy, I'm going to tell you every morning how much I love you."

After a few weeks, life got in the way and my praying the rosary became more of a weekly thing, and then a special occasions kind of thing. As I write this, it's been 2,753 days since Frank made his promise to me. On every single one of those days, Frank has texted me to tell me how important I am to him, how much he loves and appreciates me. When he knows I'm going through a tough time, he sends an inspirational quote or Bible verse to help me stay positive. In those seven-plus years I've had my ups and downs, but the one constant throughout it all has been Frank's daily text saying how much he loves me. (I think Frank says he loves me more than my wife does!) I can't put into words how much that daily investment has meant to me.

Owning your words goes a lot further than simply keeping your promises. It also means assuming responsibility when no one else will. Whenever I nail a pothole in my car, I think angrily, *Man, someone ought to do something about that.* When I pass a homeless person on the street, I think, *Someone ought to help him out.* When I walk by a bunch of trash on the beach, I think, *Someone ought to clean that up.* Too often, it's someone else's problem—not mine. There's a reason we utter that phrase so much: We don't want that someone to be us. When we say "*I* ought to do something about that," suddenly we're in a position of responsibility. We're faced with owning our words.

My friend Russ Jefferies never says, "Someone ought to." If you met Russ, you'd see a normal-looking guy with a shaved head and a neatly trimmed beard. When you ask what he does, he'll say simply, "I'm an HVAC guy." Get to know him a little, and he'll roll up his sleeves to reveal ornate tattoos spiraling up from his wrists to his shoulder blades. Russ's attention to detail is legendary. When he finishes a repair, he uses Armor All—the stuff you use to protect your car's interior—on the exteriors of the compressor, furnace, and pipes so they have a beautiful shine. If you've ever dealt with an HVAC service, you know how difficult it is to get them to show up for an appointment, let alone hand-polish your furnace. Before I met Russ, the guy who handled my A/C would give me a twelve-hour window, and I was lucky if he showed up at all. Not Russ. He and his technicians show up exactly when they say they will.

But those aren't the promises that truly matter to Russ. A few years ago, a family I knew died in their sleep because the house they were renting in Aspen, Colorado, had a carbon monoxide leak. It was a terrible tragedy that made me worry I wasn't keeping my family safe. When I told Russ about it, he dropped what he was doing and came over to thoroughly check my house for combustion leaks, expired fire extinguishers, and faulty smoke and carbon monoxide detectors. It took him all afternoon. When he finished, having found numerous potentially dangerous problems, I mentioned how alarming it was that people were living with broken safety equipment without realizing it, many of whom couldn't afford someone like Russ to do an audit.

"You're right, Tommy," Russ agreed. "I ought to do something about that."

A few months later, Russ founded Code Red Heart, an organization committed to raising awareness of hidden home dangers caused by toxic gases. Along with other volunteers, Russ performs complete home evaluations, installs carbon monoxide and smoke detectors, replaces fire extinguishers, and searches for gas leaks—all free of charge for veterans, the disabled, and really anyone who needs special assistance. For Russ, the work is personal. In 2016, he was diagnosed with multiple sclerosis, an unpredictable disease that disrupts the flow of information between the brain and the body. During MS attacks, you can lose your balance, coordination, vision, and memory, among other issues that make living alone extremely dangerous. For folks with conditions like MS, a properly functioning ventilation system can mean the difference between life and death.

Russ sacrifices a lot of his time ensuring that Denver's neediest residents are safe in their homes. Despite him having less of the week to devote to his for-profit business, it's still growing exponentially. The simple reason is that customers see the sacrifices he is making every day and say: "I want *that* guy working on my home." When the association that manages my downtown office complex needed to hire a new company to manage its hundreds of HVAC units, they chose Russ without question.

If you find that life is getting in the way of your commitments, take a page out of my friend Scott Lynn's influencer playbook. Whenever I need advice or mentorship, Scott is there for me. He's taught me more about business than any textbook or MBA degree ever has. Every time we have lunch, Scott brings along a little black notebook. In it he writes down every promise he makes to people, whether it's making an introduction, contributing to the National Leadership Academy's scholarship program, or sending me a copy of the book he's reading. He writes down every promise, no matter how small. I've known Scott for more than two decades, and he has never once failed to do what he says. Not once.

The most important promises are the ones we make to those who are in pain. Think about how many times you've said or heard this phrase: "I'm here for you. If you need anything, let me know."

I hate, hate, *hate* that sentence. We've all said it, of course. Even I catch myself now and then. From a young age, we're inculcated with politeness. *Stay in your lane. Ask permission. Mind your own business. Ask what you can do to help.* Except, think about what you are actually telling a person in pain when you say "Let me know if you need anything." On top of their real problems, you are asking them to fret over what you might or might not be willing to do. When it comes down to it, what you are *really* saying is: "I don't really want to help you, but I'm just being polite and saying what people are supposed to say."

Instead of promising vague, unspecified help, influencers take ownership of those words and act. My friend Lee is that kind of guy. I met him years ago when Jill and I moved into our house in Denver and needed an electrician. Every time Lee came over to fix wiring or change out a light fixture, I learned a little more about his life story. Lee is one of the most decent Christians I've ever met, but I learned that it wasn't always that way. When he was younger it was all about partying and girls, but at the age of twenty-one, Lee invited God in his heart and pledged never to drink again. Twenty-seven years married to his wife, Damon, and five children later, Lee has become someone I love and admire.

He's also someone who says "I ought to help" when he sees another person struggling. When the coronavirus pandemic hit, I was effectively out of a job, like millions of other people. There wasn't much work for folks who give speeches to people packed into auditoriums. I was forced to lay off my staff, and I had a serious cash flow issue after having to refund many client deposits. One morning I received a phone call from Lee. "Tommy," he said, "I just wanted to check in to see how you are doing. I know the pandemic has hurt your business. You've had a huge impact on my life and my kids' lives. My company has expanded, and my business is off the charts right now with everyone working from home. I'd like to make a deposit for my son and me to attend one of your Heart-Led Leader retreats— whenever it may happen. And I'd like to make a separate donation to the National Leadership Academy." I was stunned. During the pandemic, most people were living in fear, asking for refunds, and conserving cash. Lee, on the other hand, was writing checks and giving away his money to charitable causes.

Think back to some of the tougher times in your life. Were you influenced by the people who offered to do something for you? Or were you influenced by the ones who actually did something for you? Your stadium isn't going to be filled with people who remember the promises you made. It will be filled with people who remember the promises you *kept*. As my wife says, "Doing what you say is more important than saying what you do!"

Here's what I challenge you to do the next time you talk to someone who is going through a tough time. Instead of saying "If there's anything I can do," say "Here's what I'd like to do for you." If it's bringing over groceries to a sick friend, you say: "I'm running out to the store later today. What do you need, and when should I bring it by?" If it's visiting a grieving friend, you say: "If it's okay with you, I'd love to stop by to give you a hug. When is a good time?" If it's a new mom who is constantly exhausted, you say: "I'd really like to bring by a carton of diapers and watch the baby so you can get some sleep. When should I come?" Be specific. Be direct. And the next time you are going through a tough time, if someone tells you, "Let me know if I can do anything," let them know what it is. Don't be afraid to ask for help. You're honoring them by accepting their help, and it will surely take your relationship to the next level.

So far we've discussed the power of owning your words as they relate to promises. But there is a second way to own your words that involves a lot more than simply doing what you say. Taking ownership of your words also means being mindful of the specific words you use when speaking to others. On average, we say around sixteen thousand words a day, most of them without thinking. Can you honestly remember any of the words you said yesterday? You are influencing people every day with your words without realizing it. Words can build others up or tear them down—sometimes for a lifetime. I've learned this the hard way, to the point where my wife has a saying: "Tommy, your words have made you very successful, but they have also got you in a lot of trouble."

She's right: I have that classic hot Italian temper. In the heat of the moment, I sometimes say things that I regret—words that take a very long time to heal from. A few years ago, I arrived home after a particularly brutal stretch of travel: twenty cities over three weeks all across the world. That evening we settled down for dinner and Jill asked if I would please take care of a few things around the house that I had promised to

tackle the previous month. Her tone wasn't hostile or accusa-
tory, yet I snapped: "I just got back from a huge road trip working my tail off. What have *you* done for the past month?" The
insinuation was that Jill, a teacher who sacrificed her career to
raise our children, wasn't pulling her weight. All that time she
had been running our household alone—shuttling three kids to
hockey practice, choir, and dozens of other after-school activities, cleaning the house by herself, doing all the laundry, and
getting hardly any sleep—and I actually suggested she was *lazy*.
It was one of the most awful things I've ever said. No matter
how much I wanted to take them back, no matter how wrong
I was, I now owned those words.

Somehow Jill forgave me. That is what makes her so special. Truth is, I wish I could be more like her. When someone
says a nasty thing to me, my impulse is to cut them out of my
life. Negative words get burned into my brain. I stew on them.
I use them as fuel for motivation. Almost every day I think
about my high school typing teacher, Ms. Dizzini, who told me
I would never go to college because I was "stupid." She owned
those words, even though I'm sure she regretted them later. Jill
would have let those words go; she would have given Ms. Dizzini the benefit of the doubt, thinking maybe she was having a
bad day. That kind of emotional resiliency is Jill's superpower,
but I'm not nearly as strong.

When I was growing up, my hero was my neighbor Jimmy.
He was handsome, charismatic, athletic—a total winner. I emu-
lated everything he did. I even followed him to the same university. A while back, he went through a tough divorce. I called
him almost every day as he experienced the most humbling period of his life, and we grew extremely close as he healed. Eventually Jimmy fell in love with and married a wonderful woman,

Mallory, and we embraced her like family. And then one day Jimmy sent me a text: He and Mallory were visiting Denver, and they wanted to come over for dinner. Jill and I initially agreed, but then Jimmy asked if his in-laws could come too.

I talked it over with Jill. I was home for three days after having been on the road for a month. We were both exhausted. This was our family's chance to recharge and spend quality time together before I went back on the road. We would have happily had Jimmy and Mallory over for a casual dinner, but we weren't up to hosting a formal gathering with his in-laws. I explained the situation to Jimmy over text and asked for a rain check. To my surprise, he was terribly offended. He sent me some of the most hurtful text messages that I've ever received. I was flabbergasted, I was shocked, I was sad. In the span of a few minutes, one of the most important relationships in my life had been destroyed with a few devastating words. I did forgive Jimmy, but his hurtful words will never go away.

What's the single word that influenced you down to your bones? The word that filled you with hope—or with pain? For me, that single word was "stupid." No other word has caused me more pain. It crushed my confidence for years, though it also motivated me to work harder than everyone around me. I still get a chill every time I hear it.

After hearing words like that enough times, we can let them define us. And sometimes they start owning us in return. My friend Curtis Zimmerman calls them our "scripts": powerful thoughts and beliefs that affect the way we behave from an early age. They create automatic responses and assumptions like "I'm too old to . . ." or "I'm not good enough for . . ." or "I'll never have a relationship like . . ." Scripts like these are what keep us from trying things that are new or challenging.

Just as important, they are what prevent us from making and keeping our promises. "I'll never have time to . . . ," "I'm not strong enough to . . . ," "I'm not kind enough to . . ."

For years, Curtis followed a tough script. He came from a troubled family. His mother married six times. He moved thirty-seven times. He grew up severely dyslexic—he has it even worse than I do. He had health problems that kept him in and out of hospitals for most of his childhood. Curtis's script was not pretty, and he was following it until, at eleven years old, he met Tommy. No, not me—this Tommy was a professional mime. The best in Los Angeles. Curtis saw him performing one day in a mall. He was instantly mesmerized. Curtis practiced miming for weeks and weeks until he worked up the courage to show off his robot routine to Tommy.

"You're really good," Tommy said. "Why don't you come back tomorrow?" It instantly and forever changed Curtis's script. From that point on, Curtis was an entertainer. For the next thirty years, he traveled the world working as a mime and juggler before getting into motivational speaking. Every year for the past decade, Curtis has been a featured speaker at the National Leadership Academy. Now, trust me when I say that high school kids have the best BS detectors in the world. If you get up on a stage and aren't authentic, if what you're saying is bogus, these kids will sniff you out faster than they can say your name. With Curtis, it's not just the juggling and the fire breathing and the other tricks he does to warm up his audience; he has the rare ability to command a stage the moment he walks out there. More than any other speaker I've met, his beautiful words linger in your mind.

As Curtis always says, words do not have to tear people down. If you choose your words carefully, if you take ownership of their power, you can help rewrite another person's script. When I first heard him say that, I immediately thought back to October 18, 1986—the day my life changed forever. My high school football team, Suffern, was playing our arch-rival, Clarkstown North. We were down by two, it was fourth down, and we had the ball on Clarkstown's twenty-yard line with twenty-nine seconds left in the game. Our head coach, Bob Veltidi, had two options: have our star quarterback throw a post route to the corner of the end zone, or have the junior placekicker, who had never attempted a field goal in his entire career, go for a thirty-seven-yarder. That placekicker was me, and Coach Veltidi didn't waver for a second.

A few moments later I found myself alone on the field star-ing at the goalposts. I had never even practiced a field goal that long before. Just as I mustered some confidence, the Clarks-town coach called time out to ice me before we could snap the ball. Now I had another sixty seconds to envision all the ways I could fail. *The ball goes wide left. Or wide right. It bangs off the upright. It falls five yards short. Or worst of all . . . I whiff entirely.*

I will never forget the next sixty seconds for as long as I live. Coach Veltidi walked out onto the field and met me on the twenty-six-yard line. He grasped me by the helmet and then whispered into my ear: "I believe in you, Tommy. And whether you make this field goal or not, I'm going to love you." And then he walked calmly back to the sideline as the play clock restarted.

Suddenly the uprights looked a lot closer, and the stakes seemed a lot lower. No matter what, I was loved. A second later the center snapped the ball. The holder spun the laces. I took four steps forward and kicked the ball, just as I had done thou-sands of times in practice.

"The kick is *good*! The kick is *good*! Spaulding just snuck it over the crossbar!" the announcer screamed. "Suffern wins by one!"

That moment was more than thirty-five years ago, and I think about it almost every day. I also thought about it on December 27, 2021, when I heard that Coach Veltidi had passed away at age seventy-four. With those simple words—"I believe in you, Tommy"—he had flipped my script. He helped me see something in myself that I did not know was there, and I am forever indebted to him.

When I hear Curtis speak, I also think back to another day: November 6, 1975. I was just six years old. After having my sister Lisa and me, my parents decided to adopt an eight-month-old baby girl from South Korea. It was a bold and beautiful thing to do at a time when adoption was not as accepted as it is today.

One morning my mother said, "Tommy, we're driving to the airport today to pick up your new baby sister!"

"Great!" I said. "Is that how babies are made?"

"Yes, Tommy," she replied, holding back laughter. "You order them and pick them up at the airport!"

We arrived at John F. Kennedy Airport and—this being the 1970s—walked all the way to the gate. We were surrounded by other families, all waiting for the 747 jumbo jet from Seoul to land. Finally the gate opened, and three flight attendants walked out cradling three babies, each with a wristband matching them to their new family. When the stewardess handed my sister, Michele, to my parents, we all burst into tears. It was the most beautiful thing I had ever seen.

Then, for some reason, I decided to march up to the ticket counter and pick up the intercom. The speakers crackled, and then all the families and nurses and random passersby looked up and heard my first ever public speech: "Hi there, my name is Tommy Spaulding," I said confidently in my little pipsqueak voice. "I saw all the babies, and I just wanted you to know that my family . . . *got the best one!*"

My parents love telling that story. Michele must have heard it a million times. "We got the best one." From the day she came to the United States and joined our family, that was Michele's script. Those words had a profound impact on her development and confidence. To this day, whenever I say goodbye to my sister, I whisper: "We got the best one."

Marcus Aurelius, the Roman emperor who ruled from 161 to 180 A.D. and one of the greatest leaders and philosophers who ever lived, once said, "Perform every act of your life as if it were your last." I like to think that the very best influencers take this a step further: They speak every word as if it were their last.

Remember that words are a powerful thing. Use them responsibly.

# Start an Influence Streak

One of my most cherished places in the world is Monument Park in Yankee Stadium. It holds a collection of statues, plaques, and retired numbers honoring the best New York Yankees of all time. My favorite plaque is for Lou Gehrig, nicknamed the Iron Horse. He played first base for the Yankees from 1923 until 1939, when he became hampered by a mysterious ailment called amyotrophic lateral sclerosis. The disease, later dubbed Lou Gehrig's disease, took the Yankee great's life just two years later. When the ailing Iron Horse took himself out of the lineup in 1939, he had played an astounding 2,130 consecutive games. His plaque in Monument Park says HENRY LOUIS GEHRIG: A MAN, A GENTLEMAN AND A GREAT BALL PLAYER WHOSE AMAZING RECORD OF 2130 CONSECUTIVE GAMES SHOULD STAND FOR ALL TIME.

Indeed, for decades and decades, people thought that that record *would* stand for all time. Baseball is a tough sport. Your body breaks down when you play nine innings day in and day out. But fifty-six years after Gehrig played his last game, the streak was beaten by a shortstop named Cal Ripken, Jr. For 2,632 straight games, Cal strapped on his cleats and showed up for work. He showed up when he was sick, when his knee hurt, when anyone else would have slept in. Cal wasn't always the best player on the field in those 2,632 games. Sometimes he went 0–4 at the plate or made an error. But he always showed up, he was always dependable, and that is why he is considered one of the greatest of all time.

Streaks aren't just for baseball. Every day, someone is counting on you to simply show up, even if you aren't at your best. As Cal himself later wrote, "You raise children, you build a business, or you're there for your friends: If you just keep showing up, whether you set a record or not, you stand out—because people can count on you. Just show up."

When you think about it, showing up doesn't always feel like setting a Major League Baseball record, or making a big investment in another person. More often it feels like doing the bare minimum. It's having a decent attendance record so you can graduate from high school. It's going to weddings and funerals. It's going to work when you're not feeling well because your team needs you. Simply put, if you aren't present in the lives of others, how can you expect to have a positive influence on them?

I decided long ago that I would become the Cal Ripken, Jr. of showing up for friends and family who are going through a tough time. I wanted that streak to become my legacy. When my best friend from high school, Corey, got divorced a few years ago, I called him every day for a year. I told him he was a good man and that he would get through this. Sometimes we talked about the divorce and sometimes we did not. Sometimes Corey needed to vent his anger, and sometimes he talked about something he was looking forward to. Sometimes we went deep, and sometimes we argued about football. I learned a lot about the healing process during our daily calls. There is no magic bullet to help someone feel better. It takes time and constant presence, and that is what showing up is all about. It's not always the words that matter, but the consistency of those words.

When you show up, it's your presence that matters above everything else. Simply *being there,* even if it's a phone call, can impart an incredible amount of influence, especially in very tough times. A few summers ago, my friend Scot lost his teenage son, Teddy, to suicide. He had been the victim of horrendous cyberbullying. Scot had no idea how much pain his son was in until it was too late. I knew Teddy. He was a great kid with a great heart. Scot was in shock for months after Teddy's death, and his friends struggled with how to show up for him. What can you possibly say to someone who lost a child? I had no idea either, but I rang him up anyway and told him I loved him. I texted him every day. Above all else, I remained a presence in Scot's life. After a few months, he sent me a handwritten note that said simply: "Thank you for showing up, Tommy. I love you, too."

If you've ever gone through a tough period, you know how isolating it can feel, as if you're in a dark cave and can't see the way out. Except, every time someone shows up for you, a small light comes on and you can see a little better. If they show up again and again, the cave gets brighter and less scary. Before long, the path out is fully illuminated. Showing up for someone in this way—turning on one little light at a time—requires a streak of one small act after another. Most important, like any streak, it means being a hundred percent consistent. If you decide to show up for someone going through a tough time, pick an interval, whether it's once per day or once per week, and stick to it. Add it to your calendar if you need to.

Here's an example of what I mean. I'm friends with a wonderful couple from Fairfield, Iowa, named Lori and Nate. A few years ago, Lori, the CEO of a plastics manufacturing company, hired me to speak at the annual Iowa Association of Business & Industry. We became fast friends after she attended my leadership retreat, and I quickly fell in love with Nate, the head varsity football coach of the local high school. Lori and Nate are like the co-mayors of their little town, constantly giving back to their community and supporting local charities.

Shortly before Memorial Day weekend in 2018, Lori was diagnosed with breast cancer. The entire town rallied behind her, but the weekly chemotherapy sessions were draining. She had to wake up every Monday morning at six and drive two hours to Des Moines for her sessions. She lost her hair, and it took every ounce of her energy to leave the house every day, let alone run a major company.

Every Monday morning for twelve weeks, I called her at seven o'clock, when she would be driving to her weekly chemo session. Even when I wasn't feeling well or I wanted to sleep in, I maintained my streak because I knew Lori was looking forward to that call, to that next little light turning on inside her cave. We talked about her kids, her work, her husband's football games—anything to keep her mind off cancer. Blessedly, the treatment worked, and Lori is now cancer-free. But in a cruel twist of fate, Nate was diagnosed with testicular cancer not long after Lori finished her treatment. So I called Nate every Monday morning at seven o'clock during his drive to Des Moines. When I spoke at Lori's company not long ago, she introduced me to her employees not as a leadership expert or a bestselling author but as the friend who called her and Nate every Monday morning during the darkest period of their lives. Finally, it's not just folks going through a tough time who need you to show up for them. My relatives Doug and Susan Stanton have mastered this concept better than anyone else I know.

One of my biggest regrets about being on the road so many days of the year is that I can't see every one of Anthony's, Tate's, and Caroline's events. One thing all my kids have in common is that they love having family cheer them on. I'd move heaven and earth to see Tate or Anthony play hockey, or to see Caroline dominate on the field hockey pitch, but sometimes it's just not possible. So, at the beginning of every school year, Doug and Susan ask for my kids' schedules. They mark off every hockey and basketball game. Every school musical. Every dance recital. Then they show up—every time. Like Cal Ripken, Jr., they're famous for never missing a game. The influence they pass on to my kids isn't life-changing advice. Rather, with their simple actions, Doug and Susan are telling my children that they matter. That they are loved. That family will always be there for them. Doug and Susan understand that in so many of life's most important moments, your presence is the single greatest gift you can offer.

What's your streak? Who are the people you reliably show up for again and again? When you invest in the lives of others by showing up—every time, no matter what—your legacy will become every bit as important as Cal Ripken's.

# Be an Angel Investor

One of the most influential figures in my life is a guy I met for only a few seconds. This was back in 2005, when I was still CEO of the nonprofit Up with People. I was speaking at a conference in San Diego sponsored by Rare Hospitality, which was then the parent company of the Capital Grille and Longhorn Steakhouse.

After my talk, Jill and I were touring the venue, the Hotel Del Coronado, a gorgeous Victorian-style beach resort sitting on the San Diego Bay. As we climbed the grand steps into the lobby, we ran into Phil Hickey, the CEO of Rare Hospitality. He thanked me for talking at the event and I introduced him to Jill, who was pregnant with Caroline. We chitchatted for a minute before Jill asked Phil about his family. Phil broke into a big smile and proudly revealed that he and his wife had just celebrated their fortieth wedding anniversary. He talked about his kids and how they all lived near him in Atlanta, and how important it was to remain close to your family as you age.

Jill and I looked at each other. We both loved our parents deeply, but we didn't necessarily "do life" with them. We saw them at Christmas, Easter, Thanksgiving, maybe a birthday here or there. We called them every couple of weeks. We did everything you're supposed to do as a family, but Phil's advice made us realize how distant our connection had become. I looked at Jill's belly and wondered, *Is that how our future kids will see us? Will we live so far apart that we have to rely on bank holidays to bring us together?*

"How do you do it?" Jill asked Phil. "How do you do life together like that?"

Phil checked his watch—he had a million places to be. But the strong, gray-haired CEO regarded us with a discerning look. Then he said something I'll never forget: "You have to make your kids feel, from the second they come out of the womb until they graduate from college and start their lives, that they are one hundred percent loved unconditionally. No matter what they do. They will test you in every possible way. They will bring you to the edge. But you must love them, and more important, they must know that you love them. No matter what. That's it."

And then Phil walked away.

I've read all the books about raising kids. I've listened to dozens of eloquent podcasts about how to be a better father. But Phil Hickey's words on the steps of the Hotel Del Coronado remain the most important parenting advice I've ever received. Over the years we've had plenty of blowups with our children, like any family. We've been tested and pushed to the breaking point. But no matter how angry and upset our children make Jill and me, we always look at each other and think, *Remember Phil and the staircase conversation.* We take a deep breath and tell our kids how much we love them. No matter our faults as parents, our kids know one indelible fact: They are loved unconditionally. Nothing they do can change that. Even though we spent only three minutes with Phil Hickey, he used those three minutes to make a huge investment in my life.

Isn't it funny how sometimes the briefest interactions stay with us forever? Everyone has a story about a person like Phil. Maybe it was a teacher who introduced you to a book that changed your life. Maybe it was the stranger at the restaurant who picked up your tab. The hiring manager who gave you the job that turned into a career. Even the guy who gave you his umbrella during a downpour. You never know how even the tiniest gesture can radically change a life.

Folks like these are often called "angels," but I like to think of them as *angel investors*. In the finance world, an angel investor is someone who provides seed money for a start-up company long before other investors are willing to jump onboard. It's a very risky investment, since most start-ups fail at this stage. The term originally comes from Broadway theater, when "angels" would give money to musicals on the verge of shutting down. Some angel investors give money to a company hoping for a big return, but others do it because they believe in the leadership's vision and their potential to help the world. I like to think that influence works in a similar way. It's why people like Phil Hickey invest in the lives of strangers even though they will not get anything back.

I've been fortunate to receive many such angel investments. My business professor at East Carolina University was a gentleman named Jack Karns. He taught hundreds of students each year and didn't have time to get to know them individually. But that didn't stop him from pulling me aside one day after class. "Tommy," he said, "I noticed you biting your nails. That is a terrible habit. If you want to be respected as a business leader, you need to stop." This was a guy I had never talked to one-on-one before, yet he cared enough about my future to confront me. A few weeks later, Jack took me shopping for my first business suit and taught me that it didn't matter how much my clothes cost, only that they fit and were coordinated. So many of my painstakingly cultivated habits can be traced back to Jack, who simply cared enough to teach me how to be a man.

The key to being an angel investor is not expecting anything in return for your kindness. When you do expect something in return, you turn into a debt collector, not an investor. Several years ago, I was mentoring a talented young man from St. Louis named Ben, who was starting a brand marketing consulting firm. As he developed his curriculum, he offered to visit my office and give my staff a primer on branding. He spent the day with us and did an excellent job. A week later, Ben gave me a call. "So, Tommy," he said, "I helped you. Now what are you going to do to help me?"

In that moment, all the kindness he had shown me and my team evaporated. I realized that he hadn't invested in us because he was genuinely interested in helping; he did it to extract an IOU. Ben eventually apologized and I forgave him, but we've barely spoken since that moment. Some negative influence just cuts too deep.

Sometimes angel investors make one-time payments; other times they keep investing again and again and again. When I first moved to Denver back in 1999 to start my youth leadership development nonprofit, I had zero money and zero connections. I had no idea where to start. I was lucky enough to meet a man named Bill Graebel. When I shared with him my vision to build a program to inspire youth to become heart-led leaders, Bill didn't demand to meet my board of directors, or see my program curriculum, 501(c)(3) confirmation letter, or line-by-line spending plan. He simply said, "I'm in."

We've had more than ten thousand kids graduate from our National Leadership Academy since then, and Bill has helped bankroll the development of every one of them. If a low-income kid from the inner city can't afford the program fee, Bill will pay the full cost. When I'm planning a Global Youth Leadership Academy program in another country, Bill offers the services of his business, Graebel Relocation Services, a highly successful corporate relocation firm that handles global logistics. Anything we need, Bill is there to provide. For over twenty years, Bill has never said the word "no." Never once has he ever expected anything in return—only that I pay his kindness forward to another person whenever I can.

I thought of Bill a few years ago when my pal Scott and his wife, Kristen, called me on the phone. They were concerned about their fifteen-year-old daughter, Taylor. She was struggling with social anxiety and low self-esteem. After school she would come straight home—no activities, no hobbies, no hanging out with friends. She used to love singing, but she had stopped that too. Scott and Kristen were understandably worried, and they were hoping that the summer program I run for high school students, the Global Youth Leadership Academy, might help boost their daughter's confidence.

Of course I wanted to help, but I needed to meet Taylor first to see if she would be a good fit. A few days later, Jill and I joined Scott, Kristen, and Taylor for dinner at a local restaurant. I spent the meal pouring into Taylor, asking her meaningful questions, pushing her comfort zone, and trying to understand her world. At first Taylor was guarded, but slowly she opened up.

"Your parents mentioned that you used to love singing," I said gently. "How come you stopped? I'm sure your friends and family would love to hear your voice."

Taylor immediately crossed her arms and hunched her shoulders, as if retreating into her shell. "I don't like singing in front of other people," she murmured. "And anyway, I'm just not very good." She looked down at her food. "No one wants to hear me sing."

"Well, I'd be afraid to perform in front of people too," I replied. "Although I can tell that you have a much better voice than I do. And I know for a fact a lot of people would love to hear you sing again."

We spent the rest of the evening building trust, and then Scott and Kristen invited Jill and me to come back to their house to share some great wine. Having spent the evening with Taylor, I realized that she was a lot tougher than she seemed. She had a wicked sense of humor, and I could tell that deep down she was craving a challenge.

In Scott and Kristen's living room, I took Taylor aside and asked if she wanted to participate in our Global Youth Leadership Academy in Switzerland the following summer. She stared at me for a moment before breaking into a huge smile—the kind her parents hadn't seen in years.

"There's only one catch," I said. "You have to sing a song for us tonight."

Taylor tensed up immediately, and I feared that all the trust I had built with her had dissipated. "I . . . I need to think about it for a little while," she stammered before retreating to her bedroom.

Scott, Kristen, Jill, and I sat in the living room, chatting anxiously. What if Taylor didn't come back out? Had I pushed her too far? My job is to help teens build confidence—had I just made this young woman feel even worse about herself?

Twenty minutes later, we heard footsteps. Taylor strode into the living room, nervous but determined, and took a deep breath. Kristen clutched her husband's hand as Taylor launched into a beautiful aria. I gasped. This was the same young woman who could barely look me in the eye hours earlier, whose social anxiety had prevented her star from shining. Her long, graceful arms were no longer crossed and closing her off to the world; she now held them out proudly as she belted every note. Taylor owned that room, and Scott, Kristen, Jill, and I were all in tears.

When finished, Taylor said quietly, "Mr. Spaulding, can I join you in Switzerland now?"

The next day, Scott reached out to me. He could barely contain his joy: Taylor had not stopped singing since the previous night. It was like watching a butterfly emerge at long last from her cocoon. Taylor has flourished and gone her own way since traveling to Switzerland with our Global Youth Leadership Academy. I'm not a mentor to her the way Jerry Middel is to me. My role was to provide a one-time angel investment, and I'm honored to know it has paid dividends.

You can find simple ways every single day to make an angel investment. Sometimes the best place to start is in the workplace. About a year ago I spoke with the staff at the Players Club & Spa, a beautiful tropical retreat in Naples, Florida. During my leadership seminar, I went around the room asking everyone to tell me their name and their story. Eventually we got to a line cook named Andrean, though everyone calls her Mama. I could tell instantly that Mama was the life of the party—she's kind, fiercely loyal, and bursting with energy. She's also a single mom from Jamaica with twin boys, Tyrone and Tyrese.

"I want to tell you a story about the woman who changed my life," she said, then pointed at the general manager of the club, Denise Murphy. Mama explained that one day her son Tyrone had burst into their living room in tears. Someone had stolen his bike from the rack. When Mama went to work the next day, Denise could tell that something was off. Mama wasn't her usual buoyant self. Here's what Denise did: She asked around, and when she found out about the stolen bike, she decided to act. The next morning—on her day off—Denise drove to Walmart to make a special purchase.

"Denise texted me to come outside my apartment," Mama explained, holding back tears. "And when I got out there, Tyrone screamed with joy. She was standing beside a brand-new bike!"

I love visiting workplaces like the Players Club & Spa. They feel more like big families than for-profit companies. On that same visit, I heard story after story about how the community had come together for employees who lost their homes in hurricanes, or lost a loved one to cancer or COVID-19. There's a reason why Denise has worked there for more than two decades. There's a reason why Mama has worked there for seven years when the average tenure of a line cook is six months. It's because of everyday people finding small ways to lift one another up.

Even the smallest angel investment can pay lifelong dividends. Just ask my stepson, Anthony, who received a priceless gift when he graduated from high school a few years ago.

I was tremendously proud of Anthony. He graduated cum laude and was assistant captain of his varsity hockey team. (I, on the other hand, graduated as assistant captain of summer school.) When most kids graduate from high school, they might get a watch, an iPhone, a used car, noise-canceling headphones, or just cold hard cash. There's nothing wrong with presents like that, but Jill and I decided to give Anthony a gift that had deeper meaning.

We hatched our plan the previous summer, when I sent a letter to eight mentors who had changed my life with their influence: Jimmy, Walt, Frank, Byron, Tim, Doug, Jerry, and Scottie. "I would be honored if the eight of you would be Anthony's high school graduation gift," I wrote. "Will you each take one month of the upcoming school year and pour into Anthony?"

All eight agreed. Some of them barely knew Anthony, but that didn't stop them from going deep and investing in him, whether it was talking to him over the phone, writing him letters, mailing him inspirational books, even flying in from across the country to take him to lunch and a baseball game. I have no idea what they talked about; their conversations were strictly confidential. Each month, Anthony had the privilege of being mentored by one of the greatest influencers I know—none of whom expected anything in return.

When Anthony's graduation day came, all of these men traveled to Denver to gather for a very special dinner. All night Anthony sat at the head of the table while his angel investors stood up, one by one, and shared their final thoughts about adulthood. About becoming a man. About living a life of influence. These men came from very different backgrounds, but that didn't stop them from laughing and crying and breaking bread together like family—united by their desire to help a young man live his best possible life. Anthony stayed quiet for most of the meal, listening intently as these men poured their hearts and souls into him. Finally, when everyone had spoken, Anthony rose, looked each of his mentors in the eye, and explained exactly what he had learned from them and how it had altered his life. By the time he stopped talking, there wasn't a dry eye in the room.

After that dinner, these mentors traveled back to their own homes and their own families. It's possible that some of them will never see Anthony again. But though their time with him was short, they invested everything they had to offer in this young man—and that legacy will stand the test of time. Watches and headphones break. Cars wind up in the scrap heap. Smartphones become obsolete after a year or two. The gift of influence, on the other hand, is forever.

Who have you invested in lately? Being an angel investor does not require a massive time commitment. It simply involves telling yourself, *I'm going to help another person, even just for a few minutes, and I'm not going to expect anything in return.*

# PART IV

# The Third *I* of Influence: Intent

# It Cuts Both Ways

I always dread flying to Tucson, Arizona. I have nothing against the city itself—it's a beautiful place filled with beautiful people. It's getting off the plane that gives me anxiety.

That's because next to the Southwest Airlines gates at Tucson International Airport is the men's room. As far as airport bathrooms go, it's actually pretty nice. It has blue mosaic tile on the walls and clean stalls. Yet for nearly four years of my life, I would fly into Tucson with a knot in the pit of my stomach. When the plane descended and I felt the landing gear extend, that knot became a ball of dread, burning away at my insides like acid. By the time the plane touched down, I was in the middle of a full-blown panic attack. When we reached the gate, I'd jump up from my aisle seat, grab my bag, and sprint off the plane to that bathroom I knew so well. Then I would open one of those lovely clean stalls and puke my guts out.

I no longer have panic attacks on the plane, but I still have waves of PTSD in that airport. This is all because of one man's influence on me. This man taught me how to be a leader, and, just as important, how not to be a leader. He represents the incredible power of influence, how it can build you up and how it can tear you down. That's the thing about influence: Sometimes it cuts both ways. It's not always all good or all bad, but sometimes a shade of gray somewhere in between. In my case, the very same man who did so much good in the world was corrosive toward the people helping him reach his vision. You probably know someone like that in your life, a person who has done so many good and bad things that you can't figure out how the equation balances out in the end.

During my senior year of high school, my friends were getting accepted to great schools like Michigan, Cornell, and Harvard. They were graduating summa cum laude and magna cum laude. I, on the other hand, with my 2.0 GPA, was lucky to hang on with a thank-God-almighty cum laude. Then, at the end of my senior year in 1987, something happened that completely changed the trajectory of my life. A global youth leadership and musical organization called Up with People came to my high school to perform. They were world-famous, having sung and danced at four Super Bowl halftime shows. It was like nothing I had ever seen before. On the stage were over a hundred young people of every color, faith, creed, and nationality. Israelis and Palestinians, Indians and Pakistanis, capitalists and communists, Christians and Jews and Muslims and Hindus and Buddhists. They were all singing rock 'n' roll, smiling, laughing, and dancing together. I, on the other hand, was an Italian-Irish Catholic kid from upstate New York who had been out of state only a handful of times. Watching Up with People was the first time I realized there was an entire world out there waiting for me. And here it was in my high school auditorium.

After the show I walked up to the stage to learn about the history of the organization, which was founded in the 1960s by J. Blanton Belk. Belk had seen the ability of young people to reach across borders, see beyond race, and build bridges of understanding between people. Born from a summer youth conference in 1965, Up with People had blossomed into a worldwide phenomenon, bringing together people of vastly different mindsets, cultures, ethnicities, and beliefs through the power of music.

"Would you like to fill out an application?" one of the staff members asked me.

"Absolutely," I replied. I had never wanted to be part of something more in my life. Six weeks later I received a letter in the mail. Out of thousands of applications, I was one of just five hundred kids from around the world who had been accepted to join the group. Up with People didn't care that I was lousy at math or that I had trouble reading. They wanted me for the quality of my character, not my SAT scores. Receiving that acceptance letter was the happiest day of my life. I had it framed, and I cherish it to this day.

At seventeen years old, I stepped on an airplane for the first time and flew to Up with People's world headquarters in Tucson to meet with students from around the globe. We spent six weeks learning everything about the organization—the music, the choreography, how to become a goodwill ambassador. And then we were off to change the world. Living with a hundred host families in a hundred cities over the course of a year. Helsinki, Brussels, Stockholm, Amsterdam, Hamburg, Luxembourg—each day brought infinitely more diversity than I had known for the first seventeen years of my life. Mysterious new languages, fascinating people, strange customs, new cultures. I made dear friends from dozens of countries that year, many of whom I remain close with to this day.

After we arrived back in Tucson, my group—Cast D—had the privilege of meeting Blanton, or Mr. Belk, as everyone called him. We packed into a sweltering lecture hall at the University of Arizona to meet the man who had so deeply touched all our lives. Despite the desert heat, Mr. Belk wore a navy-blue blazer without a drop of sweat on him. His wavy hair was perfectly combed back, and when he smiled, he looked like John F. Kennedy's twin. The room of chattering teens and twentysomethings hushed when he stood. Then Blanton launched into an eloquent speech that challenged us to bring peace to every corner of the globe. To unite people through the power of song and dance. To love and serve our host families and build relationships with people of all colors and creeds. We were floored. To this day I model all my speeches on the one he delivered that hot day in Tucson.

After he finished, we hooted and hollered for what seemed like an eternity. Finally he motioned for us to quiet down. Then he asked, "Does anyone have any questions?"

Before I even knew it, my hand was in the air. "Mr. Belk," I said awkwardly, "can I shake your hand?"

Blanton smiled broadly and walked over to my seat, looked me firmly in the eye, and shook my hand. I'll never forget that moment. Then I asked him: "Mr. Belk, have you ever thought about running for president of the United States? The country needs someone like you more than ever."

The audience burst into applause. Blanton blushed and thanked me for the compliment. "Let's keep in touch," he whispered.

Throughout college we exchanged letters. He'd tell me about the latest country he had flown to, the kings and queens he had dined with. The prime ministers, presidents, and generational leaders he had visited. He inspired me to confront the ingrained racism that lingered at my college. Even as late as the 1990s there were all-white fraternities and all-black fraternities. When I became president of my chapter, I became close friends with my counterpart at the black fraternity, and we began hosting socials together for the first time in the history of the university. I even successfully ran for senior class president—something I would never have dreamed of doing without Blanton there to support me every step of the way.

As I blossomed at my career as a salesman at IBM, Up with People began a long decline. By the mid-2000s, it was on life support. Long gone were the Super Bowl halftime shows; the NFL wanted the biggest names in pop music, not kids jamming out to Chubby Checker, Motown, and the Beach Boys. But I never stopped thinking about the organization that had changed my life. One day, Blanton, now an old man, called me on the phone. "Tommy," he said, "it's time to bring music back to the world. I'm going to relaunch Up with People, and I want you to be the one to lead it."

I was speechless. I loved and venerated this man, and now he had handpicked me, at the tender age of thirty-five, to run the organization he had founded and led for nearly forty years. I couldn't say no. When Blanton introduced me as the new CEO and president to thousands of alumni in Tucson later that year, he summoned that old charisma I had spent my life emulating. "I named Tommy CEO just recently," he said, "but in truth, I decided he would be CEO nearly twenty years ago, when he was seventeen and asked to shake my hand. I looked him in the eye and knew that he would be running Up with People one day. And here we are."

As Blanton beckoned me to the stage, I hugged him and thanked him for everything he had done. The greatest man I had ever known was passing the torch to me, and I was bursting with pride. I approached the podium and delivered the most important speech of my life. I spoke from the heart. Up with People was everything to me, I said, and we needed to do everything possible to save it. I got emotional as I recalled how the organization's influence had turned me, an insecure teen with a 2.0 GPA, into the man I was today. I looked across the room at Jill, who was breastfeeding our infant daughter, Caroline. I apologized for mistakes the organization had made that had led to its decline and current financial situation. I promised to do right by our donors.

I've given thousands of speeches over my career, but this one remains the best. I left everything on that stage. When I finished, tears streaming down my cheeks, the crowd exploded into applause. I was ready to get to work and change the world.

When I got backstage, Blanton stepped in front of me. I could practically see smoke billowing from his ears. "I *never* want to see you apologizing for anything I or my organization did," he said slowly, each word dripping with derision. "It's weak to admit to your mistakes."

I stared at the man I had loved for my entire adult life. His face was twisted into something I had never seen before. "Yes, sir," I sputtered. I felt like I was seventeen again, being scolded by my dad for staying out too late.

As with any verbally abusive relationship, it was never all bad. We visited over one hundred cities around the world, tracking down alumni in the farthest reaches of the globe to raise money and share our vision for the twenty-first century. Throughout it all, I saw people look at Blanton the way I used to look at him. I saw flashes of the man I loved, the man who had changed the world with unity and music. But when no one was looking, I saw a different side to him. I was constantly bracing for the cutting remark, the explosive temper. I developed a terrible ulcer. I puked in that airport bathroom every time I came to Tucson, knowing Blanton was about to eviscerate me for some perceived wrongdoing. Most of all I was heartbroken that the man who had been such a positive influence in my life, who I believed with all my heart wanted me to succeed, was using his power to control me. To keep me in my place.

After three years as CEO, I resigned. I used the skills I had learned at Up with People to start my own leadership non-profit, and the rest is history. Six years later, I was in Tucson giving a speech. On a whim, I decided to visit Blanton's house. When he opened the door, I barely recognized him. He was in his nineties and frail. But then I saw his eyes—the same eyes that had seen something in me on that hot day in 1987. He smiled and let me in, and we sat down in his living room and shared a bourbon. We reminisced about old times. We laughed and cried. Finally I looked him in the eye and thanked him for changing the world. I thanked him for changing my life. I thanked him for helping me become the man I am today. Then we shook hands one final time, and I left. I never looked back.

In retrospect, my feelings about Blanton are complicated. He clearly was one of the most influential figures in my life. But influence can cut both ways. He believed in his organization's vision, but not in the people working to realize that vision. He taught me to see the best in people, and he also taught me to see the worst in people. But in the end he taught me about the very nature of influence itself. You can say all the right things, meet all the right people, start the very best organizations, raise millions of dollars—but if your vision never extends beyond your own periphery, you have nothing. Your influence ends not with a bang but with a whimper.

And that's why the third *i* of influence is intent. Without positive intent, truly investing in the lives of others is impossible. Intent is about asking why. *Why* are you choosing to lead others? Is it for recognition? For praise? For approval? For money? Or is it because you truly want to serve others and see them succeed? Put another way, while the first two *i*'s of influence are about earning your influence, intent is about maintaining that influence for the long term.

In this section, I challenge you to think about the concept of *legacy*. Many people think about their legacy in terms of accomplishments. You made this much money, achieved this title, founded these many companies, and so on. But true influencers have a different way of thinking about legacy. They see it in terms of how many people they developed into leaders—and how many people surpassed them.

Everyone knows Vince Lombardi, one of the greatest head coaches in NFL history. He coached the Green Bay Packers during the 1960s, leading the team to five NFL championships and two Super Bowls. The man's name is so synonymous with winning that the Super Bowl trophy is named after him. Except here's something you probably don't know about Coach Lombardi: He never groomed a successor. When he died suddenly in 1970, there was no Packers coach prepared to step in and take the reins. As a result, the Packers spent years mired in mediocrity. In fact, not a single disciple of "the Pope"—as everyone called Lombardi—went on to win a championship. Not one!

Now, you might also have heard of Bill Walsh, the longtime coach of the San Francisco 49ers. He won 102 games overall, including three Super Bowls, but that's nothing compared with Don Shula's 347 wins or Bill Belichick's six Super Bowl victories (and counting). Walsh is ranked just forty-fifth all time in wins, yet many consider him the greatest coach of all time—even better than "the Pope" himself. That's because of Walsh's legacy. If you look at his "coaching tree"—all the past and current head coaches who can be traced back to him—Walsh has no equal. Unlike Lombardi, Walsh poured his energy into his assistants so that they might one day go on to coach their own winning teams. As he wrote in his autobiography, "The ability to help the people around me self-actualize their goals underlines the single aspect of my abilities and the label that I value most—teacher." So far, Walsh's legacy includes dozens of head coaches, many of whom have gone on to win championships of their own. Close to half of all Super Bowl teams since 1981 have been coached by either Walsh or a member of his tree. Walsh may be ranked only forty-fifth in wins, but he's number one where it counts most.

My friend Joe Krenn is a guy who puts Walsh's philosophy into practice every single day. He's one of the most successful general managers in the country. Except he isn't a football GM—Joe runs a country club, which in many ways requires more management and interpersonal skills than an NFL franchise. Under his direction, Farmington Country Club in Charlottesville has become one of the most financially successful institutions in the country. He took over the club when it was deep in the red and hemorrhaging members during the depths of the Great Recession, its centuries-old buildings quite literally falling apart. Joe completely turned around Farmington's culture, attracted new members, embarked on a multi-million-dollar renovation, and restored the club to profitability. Five years into his tenure, he won the Club Managers Association of America award for top general manager in the country.

But these aren't the numbers Joe cares about. Rather, it's the number of his former employees who have gone on to become leaders in the country club industry. For Joe, that number is sacred. It's his influence tree. I've met many of the men and women who were hired by Joe as college interns. For years he poured into them, invested in their careers, and watched as they went on to become general managers, directors, and clubhouse managers—both at Farmington and at competing clubs. In the end, Joe sees his workplace not as a country club but as a leadership development organization.

As we'll see in this section, the very best influencers think like Bill Walsh and Joe Krenn. They follow the words of Eleanor Roosevelt, who once said, "A good leader inspires people to have confidence in the leader; a great leader inspires people to have confidence in themselves." These leaders plant seeds and cultivate sprawling influence trees. They may go on to great accomplishments themselves, but they measure their success by how well they develop future leaders. And their legacy never stops growing.

# Influencers Eat Last

On a sweltering day in June 2014, a few miles outside Lowell, Massachusetts, six high-level managers from the popular grocery chain Market Basket resigned in protest. It wasn't an easy decision. For some of them, Market Basket was the only employer they had ever worked for. But this was only the first step in a weekslong odyssey that would see a multi-billion-dollar company shaken to its core. Days later, three hundred employees rallied outside the company's headquarters. Within weeks, the protests had swelled to five thousand customers and employees, all united in their support of one man who had sacrificed so much on their behalf.

Market Basket is one of the most popular supermarkets in New England, with more than eighty stores and twenty-five thousand employees. Founded as DeMoulas Market in 1917 by Greek immigrants Athanasios and Efrosini Demoulas, the store would rapidly grow into a chain of ultra-low-cost supermarkets with a rabid following. Market Basket was not the kind of place you went to buy $30 filet mignon or kombucha; it appealed to everyday folks who needed cheap staples to feed their families. By the 2000s the company was controlled by two cousins named Arthur—Arthur S. Demoulas and Arthur T. Demoulas—who represented warring halves of the family.

The feud boiled down to Market Basket's CEO, Arthur T. Demoulas, affectionately called Artie T. by his employees, and his worker-friendly practices. According to legend, Artie T. could recall the names of all his employees, their birthdays, and the names of their spouses. When the daughter of a store manager was seriously injured in a car accident, Artie called him up and asked if the hospital was doing enough. "Do we have to move her?" he asked. *We,* meaning family. He attended employee weddings and funerals, and despite the rock-bottom prices, Market Basket paid some of the most generous wages in the industry. Artie instituted a 15 percent profit-sharing system that allowed rank-and-file employees to share in the company's success, a scholarship program, and many other employee-first policies that won him a cult-like following. When the profit-sharing plan sustained a $46 million loss during the 2008 financial meltdown, Artie replenished it with company funds. Needless to say, these financial sacrifices came at the expense of shareholder value. By one account, Artie T. had diverted $300 million from Market Basket profits to his employees, which rankled his cousin, Arthur S., who wanted more cash flowing to the top.

When Artie T. attempted to earmark 20 percent of company profits for worker bonuses, Arthur S. and Market Basket's board of directors sprang into action. In June 2014, they fired Artie T. and drastically slashed the employee profit-sharing program. When the new CEO planned major cost reductions, the six high-level managers resigned, inciting a wave of protesters who believed that the board was rewarding shareholders instead of hardworking employees. The leadership threatened to fire any worker who joined the protest, but the demonstrations swelled to over ten thousand strong. Employees and shoppers alike picketed Market Basket headquarters with signs reading SAVE ARTIE T! Drivers stopped making deliveries. The story became a media sensation as public support for the workers exploded. Customers began shopping elsewhere, and within weeks of Artie T.'s firing, Market Basket sales had plummeted an astounding 70 percent. At one point the company was losing $10 million per day. Finally, Massachusetts governor Deval Patrick and New Hampshire governor Maggie Hassan helped broker a deal in which a demoralized Arthur S. agreed to sell his stake in Market Basket to his cousin Artie T. for $1.5 billion. The protesters declared victory.

What was it about Artie T. that inspired such fierce loyalty among his customers and employees? He was a good boss, obviously, but most bosses don't have a literal army of support. What separates Artie T. is one simple trait: He put the needs of his followers first, full stop, no matter what. I recognized this kind of raw, unflinching devotion a long time ago in my aunt Loralee, whom I wrote about earlier in the book, and I see it embodied by the very best influencers time and again.

My first year out of college, I was tasked with running an educational program for Up with People. It was my job to bring a group of international students to Eastern Europe. It was a life-changing trip for us. We stood beneath the iron gate at Auschwitz and understood for the first time the true meaning of evil. We ate pierogies in the Main Square in Kraków, one of the most beautiful and underrated public spaces in the world. Toward the end of the trip, we stayed with a local family in Bratislava, in what was then Czechoslovakia. Our hosts were clearly honored to have us. They didn't have much, but they brought out their best china to serve us delicious pork schnitzel and potatoes. The dinner was family-style, and I immediately grabbed two schnitzels and passed the plate along. The next morning, an eighteen-year-old student pulled me aside and gave me perhaps the greatest lessons in leadership I've ever received.

"Tommy," he said, "you probably didn't count, but there were eighteen pieces of pork on the plate and there were eighteen people at the table. You served yourself first and took two pieces. And you call yourself our leader? Leaders always eat last."

I've seen that advice proven right again and again over the years. The leaders who eat last are easy to spot because their followers can't stop gushing about them. Mike Casey, for example, eats last. He's the CEO of Carter's, a children's apparel company that was founded the same year the Civil War ended. Their various brands, which include OshKosh B'gosh, account for more than 10 percent of the young children's apparel market. Mike's been at the helm since 2008, during which time he's more than doubled the size of the business. But that's not the metric he's most proud of. Unlike most companies that routinely lay off employees to keep costs down and Wall Street happy, Carter's under Mike's leadership focuses on recognizing and rewarding its workforce of nearly twenty thousand employees, even during lean times.

Here's a story his head of human resources, my friend Jill Wilson, told me: One time Mike was visiting a distribution center when he was approached by a custodian named Richard, who proudly explained the measures he had taken to bring cleaning costs down. Richard suggested that the savings could be directed toward Carter's 401(k) program. Most CEOs would use the extra cash for stock buybacks and shareholder dividends, but that's not Mike. When he got back to his office, he handwrote Richard a note thanking him for his hard work and promised to keep the needs of employees first.

That year, and for eight of the twelve years Mike has served as CEO, Carter's has provided a 100 percent company match of its employees' 401(k) contributions, whereas most companies cap their matching contributions at a much lower percentage. In 2021, Carter's provided a special bonus of three weeks' pay and a 125 percent match of 401(k) contributions to recognize and thank its workers for enduring the challenges of the global pandemic while balancing their commitments to their families and Carter's. It's no coincidence that Carter's has one of the highest employee retention rates in the industry.

It's not just CEOs and other business leaders who eat last. My aunt Loralee never worked for a Fortune 500 company or had to make decisions that affected the jobs of thousands of people. But when rebel armies were descending on her mission in Zwedru, Liberia, my aunt refused to leave until every last man, woman, and child was evacuated. Her life has influenced not just the refugees she saved in Liberia but people like me who watched her sacrifices and pledged to be more like her.

Most important, my aunt taught me that anyone who wants to positively influence the lives of others must never stop sacrificing. It can mean sacrificing some money to give to a good cause. It can mean sacrificing your time to help a friend in need. But most of the time, it simply means sacrificing your ego in the service of others.

Here's an example. A few years ago, Jill and I took our kids to Singer Island in Florida for spring break. I struck up a poolside conversation with a guy named Ed Shaw, who shared that he had worked for twenty-five years as an insurance claims adjuster for the same company. One day Ed was called into his manager's office—on his birthday, no less—and informed that he was being let go because of downsizing. "You don't have to work the rest of the week," his boss said, "but we'll pay you until Friday." That's what Ed got after twenty-five years of dedicated service.

After being treated like that, most people would be angry. Ed's fellow laid-off co-workers certainly were; they left that day and never came back. With my Italian temper, I probably would've done the same.

Except that's not what Ed did. He had dozens of clients who needed to be carefully handed off. The company might not have been loyal to him, but Ed was loyal to his customers. For the rest of the week, Ed showed up at his desk and methodically planned his departure. He personally called every client and told them what an honor it had been to serve them. At seven o'clock on Friday evening he cleared his desk and left for the last time. The following Monday, Ed filed for unemployment compensation and began searching for a new job. A few days later he received a call from his former employer's biggest competitor. It turns out that a big client of Ed's had jumped ship and recounted to his new firm how Ed remained dedicated to his customers until the end. "We need that kind of loyalty around here," the hiring manager told Ed. "We'd love to bring you onboard."

The best influencers know that it's not enough just to serve others. You have to mean it. My mentor Jerry Middel drilled this precept into my head. He was the one who pushed me to give back to my community as I became more successful. There was just one catch: "You can't tell anyone about it, Tommy. When you give money, when you volunteer your time, as soon as you tell someone about it, it's no longer a gift, it's a tax deduction." There's nothing novel about this idea, of course. Way back in the twelfth century, Maimonides, the preeminent Jewish scholar of the Middle Ages, outlined his eight levels of *tzedakah*, or charity. The second most important principle, after always lending money to friends in need, was anonymous giving: "Give tzedakah anonymously to an unknown recipient via a person or public fund which is trustworthy, wise, and can perform acts of tzedakah with your money in a most impeccable fashion." In other words, you give because it is right, not because you want to be seen doing it.

Sometimes the effect of generous acts of service can be wiped out because your intent is not clear. For example, one of my greatest influences was my father-in-law, Ernie Delgado. The second youngest of eight kids, Ernie grew up poor in Santa Fe, New Mexico. He began working from a very early age to help support his family. Ernie learned English, studied hard to make good grades, worked and saved money, and put himself through college. When he arrived in Greeley, Colorado, he found work as a teacher despite entrenched discrimination that lingered in the area. But Papa Tiger, as everyone called him, overcame prejudice to earn a good living and support his family. I've never met a harder worker in my life. To this day, one of the best compliments Jill ever gave me was that my work ethic reminded her of her father's.

Like many self-made men and women, Ernie had a bit of an insecure chip on his shoulder. Growing up a devout Catholic and with limited resources, he was committed to helping the disadvantaged. He volunteered hours and hours for the church and organized events benefiting the less fortunate. He donated to charity and helped his neighbors. Ernie did a great deal of good for his community, and he liked people to know about it. When we had dinner with new acquaintances, he'd recount his latest donation or good deed, and I'd see the look on people's faces. They didn't necessarily know his past or his heart, and they probably assumed he was a blowhard. I knew Ernie was coming from a place of love for his community and pride for what he had overcome. A man who had to earn everything in life the hard way, he felt he had to earn his seat at the table even in his final years. I understood and loved him for that, but it broke my heart that some were not able to see the Ernie I knew—that the negative influence generated by a little bluster could overshadow such a beautiful soul. If I could go back, I'd tell Ernie something that Jerry told me: "Let others brag about your generosity."

At the end of the day, sometimes the most important sacrifice you can make is your pride. You probably remember the great arctic blast of 2021, which brought subzero temperatures to America's heartland and left millions of Texans without electricity or heat for days. When the cold front descended, I was in Nashville with my son Tate for a hockey tournament. When you think of Nashville, you probably think of country music, hot chicken, and Johnny Cash—not extreme cold and whiteout conditions. Well, after a thrilling tournament in which Tate's team beat all twelve competitors, we stepped out into a historic blizzard that brought the Music City to its knees. All flights were canceled. We made it to the airport the next day to find that our flight was still delayed because (as we learned later) the airline's deicing machine was broken. Whenever we approached the front desk, the attendant scowled and said: "We'll be boarding soon. Please be patient."

After twelve hours of sitting around hearing the same line—"We'll be boarding soon, please be patient"—the passengers started getting testy. *Why aren't you giving us any information? What are the chances we fly tonight? Do we need to book a hotel for another night? Can I get a refund?* All the other flights were taking off except for ours. The anger among the passengers was contagious. We were frustrated that we weren't boarding the plane, yes, but we were mainly angry that the airline did not apologize or own up to its broken deicing machine. They did not explain the situation or attempt to give us a realistic timetable of taking off. The airline clearly did not mean to strand us at the airport, but their lack of transparency overshadowed whatever positive intentions they might have had.

Finally, instead of apologizing, here's what the airline did: They called the cops. Yes, four uniformed airport officers showed up to guard the front desk from a bunch of hungry twelve-year-olds and hockey parents.

That story is certainly an example of truly awful customer service, but it also gets to the nucleus of how bad influence works. You see, humans essentially have two brains in one. The first is what scientists call the "what is" mind. It looks out, sees what's happening around you, and responds with gut-level emotions like excitement, sadness, and anger. When you're in the airport, the "what is" mind sees delays and gets angry because you won't get home on time. It gets happy when the flight finally boards and relieved when it lands. The second mind is the "what ought to be" mind. This part of the brain is a lot more complicated, because it sees not just what an outcome is but also how it should have looked. The "what ought to be" mind sees airport delays and thinks, indignantly, that somebody should fix the damn plane and be more communicative. This brain gets pleased or irritated based on how others are reacting to a situation. *Don't they see how this is affecting me? Why aren't they as annoyed as I am right now?*

The deepest, most lasting influence emerges in situations when your "what is" mind is upset at a situation but your "what ought to be" mind is pleased with a person's true intentions. Put another way, it's when people take the high road. A few years ago, a friend of mine—we'll call her Sue for privacy— told me an unbelievable love story that speaks to the heart of influence. She got engaged to her college sweetheart—we'll call him Mark—right after they graduated. The following fall she enrolled at Harvard Business School. She had a grueling course load, and during the semester she became close with a classmate, Dave. They spent long hours together studying for exams, doing group projects, and sharing late-night meals. Soon Sue and Dave were something more than friends; they were having an emotional affair. Wracked with guilt, Sue finally came clean to Mark.

Most guys would get angry and maybe scream terrible words. Maybe they'd break off the engagement or try to beat the other guy up. Instead, this is what Mark said: "He really must be a special guy if you have feelings for him. I'd like to meet him. Why don't you invite him over for dinner?"

I literally gasped when she told me that. Mark swallowed his pride and made his rawest, most heartfelt intention clear: He wanted Sue to be happy, no matter what. Even if that meant her being with someone else.

As you can probably imagine, the dinner was awkward. Yet Mark was a total gentleman—calm, polite, and understanding. Dave, on the other hand, was the complete opposite. He was rude, arrogant, and cocky. By the end of the night, Sue realized she had made a terrible mistake, and she fell in love again with the humble man whose reaction to her missteps was to be kind. Fast-forward twenty-five years, and Sue and Mark are happily married with a beautiful family.

When I heard this story, I couldn't help but think back all those years ago to my dinner with my host family in Bratislava, when I learned that sometimes leaders must literally eat last. But Mark showed me what it looks like to "eat last" in a bigger sense. In the end, Mark is a guy who could put Sue's interests above his own, even when every instinct was screaming at him to do the opposite. Even when it was unfair. He ate last of the dish of pride and sacrificed his ego when it mattered most. And it was that indelible influence that created one of the most rock-solid marriages I've ever known.

# Are You a Fan Hogger?

When my daughter, Caroline, was thirteen, she attended a sleepaway camp in northern Vermont near the Canadian border. It instantly became her favorite place in the world. She loved it so much that she cried when we picked her up at the end of the summer. She had made dozens of new friends and lifelong memories and begged to go back the next year.

But the next summer, that all changed. When Jill and I picked her up, she was subdued. She said goodbye to her friends and quietly got into the car. No tears, no desperate pleas to sign up for next year. When we asked how she enjoyed camp, Caroline didn't rattle off all the new friends she'd met and all the new activities she had tried. She simply said, "It was fine."

"Do you want to go back again next year?" I asked.

Caroline shrugged and looked out the window. "No, I don't think so."

It took a little while before she was ready to tell us what happened. She didn't have any problems with friends or the camp activities. It was her counselor—we'll call her Amy—who lived with Caroline and ten other campers in one of the log cabins. Caroline explained that because there was no air-conditioning in the cabin, it got very hot at night. There was a fan in the corner that normally rotated back and forth so everyone could get some relief. Instead, Amy pointed it directly at her bed. For four weeks, even when it was ninety degrees, she refused to let any of the campers share its cooling breeze. Even though Caroline loved her friends, the sports, the activities, she couldn't stop thinking about how Amy hogged the fan for herself. It soured the entire camp experience, and Caroline never went back.

When you think about it, there are fan hoggers everywhere, and most of us have seen how they can ruin an otherwise wonderful organization. Just take it from Kelsey, a young professional who attended our National Leadership Academy years ago. A remarkably bright woman, she went on to graduate from Stanford University and get a job at a very well-known Silicon Valley tech company. It was the kind of job people would kill for, with a sky-high salary, amazing perks, a positive corporate vision, and awesome co-workers. When we met for coffee one day, I was shocked to learn that Kelsey needed my help finding a new job. When I asked why she wanted to leave such a great company, she replied: "I hate my boss. He has a massive ego. He puts himself first and constantly throws his direct reports under the bus." Kelsey could spot a self-serving leader from a million miles away, and she wanted out—even if it meant leaving an otherwise stellar company.

Here's what I told Kelsey: "Most leaders are like your boss: self-serving. It's just really hard to be a servant leader."

Pop quiz: What's the number one reason people quit their jobs, according to a Gallup poll of more than a million American workers? Bad bosses. As the old saying goes, employees join companies but leave managers. That much is true, but I want to take it one step further: The negative influence of a single bad apple is often fatal. All it takes is a single fan hogger to ruin the culture of an otherwise great organization.

I'm blessed to speak to thousands of business leaders each year, and I always start off with the same question for my audience: "Who wants to have a negative influence on the lives of others?"

Not a single person has ever raised their hand. Of course not—what kind of jerk *tries* to be a bad boss?

"Fantastic," I tell my audience. "You want to be a good leader. That's the first step. You get to decide that you want to be a positive influence at every level of your organization. Unfortunately, that's about where your choices end. You get to decide the kind of influence you *want* to have on others, but you don't get to decide the influence you *do* have on others."

I scan the audience, watching them frown and scratch their heads in confusion. "You get to decide the kind of influence you *want* to have on others," I say again, slower, "but you don't get to decide the influence you *do* have on others. Who does?"

Your *followers* decide. Your spouse, your children, your employees, your customers, your clients, your neighbors, your friends—these are the people who respond to your influence and decide what kind of leader you become.

When I am brought to an organization as a leadership coach, I ask each member of the executive team one question straight up: "Do you think you're a good influence on your team?" They almost always say yes, and they truly believe it. But then something interesting happens. I survey their direct reports in confidence. I speak with the mail guys, the secretaries, the janitors, the assistants—the folks who work for these leaders day in and day out. And their responses aren't always pretty. Too often there is a gaping chasm between how leaders think of themselves and how their followers think of them. Like with Kelsey's boss, their actions do not line up with their intentions.

To illustrate this point, I have the participants in my Heart-Led Leader retreats try a simple exercise. I give each of them two sticky notes, one yellow and one blue. Then, on a white-board, I make two columns. On the left: *Good Leader*. On the right: *Bad Leader*.

"I want you to think about the best boss you've ever had," I say. "This is the person who has had the biggest influence on you, who has been the most important leader and mentor—no matter if you were flipping burgers or putting together a multi-million-dollar merger. Write down this person's first name on the yellow sticky note."

The room goes quiet. I watch the faces of these executives and managers as they run through their list of bosses. "Now, on a blue note, I want you to write down the name of the worst boss you've ever had, the one who was a terrible influence." This one doesn't take long at all—everyone remembers *that awful boss*, after all.

"Now bring your notes up and place them on the white-board."

"Everyone wants to be here one day," I say, gesturing to the yellow sticky notes. "A servant leader who always puts the needs of others first. A positive influence who is loved and re-spected by their people because of their actions, not their title. That's the goal." Then I point at the sea of blue sticky notes on the board. "I'll bet you anything these bosses wanted that too."

"Rick, Maureen, Jason . . ." I read them one by one. "Retta, Stu, Bruce—no one on this list wanted their name to end up on a blue sticky note. They set out to be a good influence like you all did today. They wanted to be a yellow-sticky-note leader.

But their *followers* decided what color note they became. Their actions and their intentions were not aligned, and they became bad influences."

I look at my audience, many of whom will be the CEOs, CFOs, and sales managers of tomorrow. They look uncomfortable. They know what question is coming. "I know what color sticky note you all *want* to be. But what color *will* you be?"

Here's the root of the problem: It can take years to earn good influence with your followers, but it takes only seconds to lose it. When you think about the blue-sticky-note bosses you've had, you remember all the bad stuff. You remember the boss who threw you under the bus. The boss who denied you time off when you were burned out. The boss who was just in it for themself. All that bad influence is burned into our minds, and we forget the good qualities that would've gotten them to a position of influence in the first place.

Truth is, negative influence sticks around for a long time, and that goes for everyone, not just bad bosses. If you're a baseball fan, you've probably heard of Bill Buckner. With two outs in the bottom of the tenth inning of game 6 of the 1986 World Series, Buckner, the Red Sox first baseman, let a lazy ground ball bounce under his glove, allowing a runner to score and handing the Mets a dramatic come-from-behind victory. Radio announcer Vin Scully's depiction is one of the most famous play calls in history: *"Little roller up along first . . . BE-HIND THE BAG! IT GETS THROUGH BUCKNER! HERE COMES KNIGHT, AND THE METS WIN IT!"* The Mets went on to win the World Series, and Buckner's name has become synonymous with futility ever since.

Here are some other things you probably didn't know about Bill Buckner: He played for twenty-two years. He received votes for Most Valuable Player on five occasions. He made the

All-Star team. In 1980 he won the batting title with a .324 average, and he compiled 2,715 hits over his career—more than Hall of Fame heroes Ted Williams, Mickey Mantle, or Joe DiMaggio. In fact, only sixty-five players in the history of baseball had more hits. Bill Buckner has better statistics than many Hall of Famers, yet he dropped off the ballot in his first year of eligibility. If not for that one error, Buckner would likely be enshrined in Cooperstown today.

Like baseball, influence isn't fair. It's a fickle, irrational thing. You can spend years and years making all the right choices to earn the trust and respect of your followers, and yet sometimes these relationships boil down to how well you react in a single moment. Do you rise to the occasion and do the right thing? Or does all that trust and goodwill slip by you like a soft ground ball until all that's left is your name on a blue sticky note?

The human brain is hardwired to hold on to negative emotions. As the psychologist and author Rick Hanson explains, "The brain is like Velcro for negative experiences, but Teflon for positive ones." It comes down to survival instincts: When you're a kid and you touch a hot stove, that memory is burned in your brain for the rest of your life. You don't remember all the times you touched a cold stove. Similarly, studies show that people will work much harder to avoid losing money than they will work to gain the same amount. The same goes for our relationships: If you are a negative influence on someone, it will take an enormous amount of work to convince the brain to let go of that negativity. A famous set of studies by the psychologists Dr. John Gottman and Dr. Robert Levenson from the 1970s found that for every negative interaction, a relationship requires five positive ones to make up for it.

Consider that for a second. For every moment of bad influence, you need five good ones to make up for it. It is a little easier to see how your name ends up on a blue sticky note when you think about it that way.

I learned this personally a few years ago. My longtime friend Bill Petrella manages the Hotel Emma, a luxurious resort in San Antonio, Texas. It's one of the most special hotels I've ever stayed at in my life. A few hundred feet away is the Culinary Institute of America, which has trained many of the chefs at Hotel Emma's three separate restaurants. The hotel is in a former brewhouse, and its design—concrete beams, exposed pipes, strange old machinery scattered about—is breathtaking.

A few years ago, Bill hired me to hold a leadership seminar with his team. In return, he invited Jill and me to be his guests for a long weekend. We flew down to San Antonio and I gave a talk to over a hundred of Bill's employees at the hotel. I explained the difference between good influencers and bad influencers. Good influencers are humble and genuine. They are loving. They are forgiving and patient. Bad influencers, meanwhile, put themselves first. They are disrespectful to others. They look down on people they consider to be beneath them. It's a talk I give regularly, and I take it very seriously.

Later that night Bill arranged to have one of his hotel cars take us to a fancy restaurant in downtown San Antonio. Owing to a miscommunication with the driver, Jill and I ended up waiting half an hour outside the hotel before the car picked us up. When the car arrived, I complained to the driver that we were late for our dinner reservation. Looking back, I don't remember what I said, exactly; people make short remarks like that all the time.

The following morning, I was at the hotel gym when Bill approached me. "Hey, Tommy," he said, taking me aside. "Look, this is no big deal, but something came to my attention this morning. One of our managers mentioned that you might have been a little bit short with the driver last night. Do you know what he's talking about?"

"I honestly don't remember, Bill," I admitted. "I think I might have commented that he was late. Is something wrong?"

"Don't worry about it. We'll take care of it. It's just that the driver may have repeated your comment to a few people, and it kind of spread among the staff."

I closed my eyes as I realized the magnitude of what I had done. This was the same staff to whom I had preached the importance of being a good influence. I had addressed over a hundred drivers, cooks, managers, housekeeping staff, and executives about why leaders need to be respectful to employees at every level of the company. "It's not about you," I had said again and again. I had written it in giant letters on the board: IT'S NOT ABOUT YOU. True influencers lead with their heart and build trust. They are mindful of every single interaction. Self-serving influencers are the opposite. They are rude and condescending. They are triggered by the smallest slights. They're the kind of people who bark at drivers for being late.

I wrote the driver an apology. I wrote the manager an apology. I wrote Bill an apology. I truly intended to do whatever it took to make things right. I desperately wanted the hotel's staff to know that the man in the car was not the man who had addressed them earlier that morning. Except it was too late. My actions failed to live up to my intentions. The staff at Hotel Emma saw a smooth-talking guy who could speak eloquently about being a good influence, but whose actions suggested he was a selfish jerk. Even though Bill has generously invited me back to speak to his team, I've never led another leadership seminar at the Hotel Emma. How could anyone there take me seriously?

No one is perfect. We all have good days and bad days. But the very best leaders are always aware of how they are treating the people around them. They realize when they are hogging the fan, and then they course-correct.

My friend Shawn Early is an example of a leader who made a few mistakes, but when it mattered most, he turned the fan around. Shawn is the classic American success story. After a difficult childhood, he became the first member of his family to graduate from college, paying his way by flipping burgers at a hole-in-the-wall diner. When I first met Shawn, he produced from his wallet a yellowing piece of paper that looked as if it had been folded and unfolded thousands of times. The ink had faded over twenty years, but I could make out a phone number. "I met my wife while working at that diner," he said proudly. "I'll never forget when she gave me her number. It was the best day of my life. I keep this with me wherever I go."

As their relationship flourished, Shawn knew he had to find a career. Through a friend, he found a job paying $10 per hour as a merchandiser for Pepsi in Amarillo, Texas. It was humble work, but Pepsi offered to pay for the rest of Shawn's college degree as he climbed the corporate ladder. Except Shawn didn't so much climb as vault, earning promotion after promotion as his responsibilities ballooned.

Eight years later Shawn was married, celebrating the birth of his second child, and settling into his role as a sales director for Pepsi in Wichita, Kansas. It was an executive-level role with big responsibilities for a guy who had been stocking shelves a few years earlier. Instead of overseeing frontline employees like the kind he used to be, Shawn was wearing a suit, managing clients, drafting regional sales plans, and making a good living. The only tokens of his humble beginnings were that folded piece of paper in his wallet and a tattered Pepsi ball cap, issued to him when he first started with the company. Now it hung proudly behind his desk.

I once asked him why he held on to that sweaty old cap. "To remind me of where I started with Pepsi," he said.

One day Shawn was called into his boss's office. Pepsi was going through a reorganization and his job was being eliminated. Would he consider staying on and taking a sales manager job? It was a big demotion. Gone were the executive perks and the suits. He'd be back in the warehouse overseeing soda deliveries. Shawn took the job, but he was angry. Who did they think he was? He had done everything right as an executive. Impressed the right people. Hit all his sales targets. Hired the right people. He was the golden boy, the prized number one draft pick. Now he was the kid who gets picked last for kickball.

A few weeks later Shawn was stewing at his desk when an employee stepped inside his office. His name was Sammy, a merchandiser. "Hey, boss," he said, holding out the handheld computer he used to make orders. "My handheld is broken. Could you help me get it working?"

Shawn looked at Sammy and felt a wave of frustration. A month ago, he had an executive role and was traveling around the Midwest. Now he was supposed to do tech support for a merchandiser?

"I don't have time for this, Sammy," Shawn said. "Please call someone whose job it is to fix these things." He was being a jerk, a self-serving boss more concerned about a career road bump than the needs of his employees.

"Okay, boss," Sammy said. Then his eyes found the old ball cap behind Shawn's desk. "Oh, I also lost the cap for my uniform. Do you know where I could get one like yours?"

Shawn felt more frustration bubbling inside him. But then

he looked over his shoulder and saw the battered hat he once wore as a merchandiser. Suddenly he felt a rush of shame. Back then, he didn't care about traveling around the market and entertaining customers. He was just grateful to have a steady paycheck. Sammy hadn't come into his office to rub that demotion in his face; he wanted his handheld fixed so he could do his job. Shawn's job was to help his employees succeed, and somewhere he had lost sight of that mission. He had become the cliché of the overly ambitious kid who was only in it for himself, and everyone could see it. He was hogging the fan.

It was as if a valve let go somewhere. All that resentment that had built up inside him drained away. For the first time in a while, Shawn understood that it wasn't all about him.

"Tell you what, Sammy," he said. "Let's go fix your handheld and find you a new hat."

From then on, Shawn had a new policy: If his team needed something, they came to him. If they wanted to advance beyond the front line and enter management, they came to him. In the process, a funny thing happened. Shawn had lost the good things—the expense account, the title, the frequent flier miles, the golf outings—but he had gained something better: a team of loyal men and women whom he considered family.

A while later, Shawn was promoted back to general manager, and today he oversees PepsiCo's Mountain West market in the United States. He's a pillar in our community, one of the greatest heart-led leaders I know. After his big promotion, I asked him what he was most proud of. He smiled at me and plucked his old cap off the wall. He ran his fingers over the rips and the sweat stains and the faded Pepsi logo. For a long time, that cap was all about Shawn—his hard work, his ambitions, his future. Now that cap meant something very different.

"I'm proud of my team, Tommy," he said. "I'm proud that

more than seventy percent of my management staff began on the front lines, just like me. Now look where they are today."

Shawn succeeded where so many other leaders fail. He had been hogging the fan, but he changed his attitude before lasting damage was done. People like Shawn are rare. I see so many people who believe that success is zero sum. They believe that to do well, others must do worse. Almost every time I do the sticky note exercise with a company, someone approaches me afterward. "Tommy, I want to be on a yellow sticky note one day," they say. "But I just don't see how that is a successful business model. Sometimes you just need to be a jerk to succeed."

That's when I tell them about one of the most successful businessmen I know. A guy who's never once hogged the fan and has made a career out of putting others first.

I've been blessed to work on the national speakers circuit for many years now. I take my speaking engagements very seriously and spend weeks preparing for each of them. I also have an important rule: I don't personally invest financially in my clients' businesses, many of which are well-established organizations, promising start-ups, and publicly traded companies. It's not just about being aboveboard and ethical; the way I see it, investing my heart and soul into my clients is far more important than investing money. In twenty-five years, I've broken my rule only once, and it was for an influencer named Jackson McConnell.

I don't know how best to describe Jackson, except to say that if you had a daughter, he would be the kind of guy you'd want her to marry one day. Born and raised in Georgia, he's got a buttery southern drawl that has the effect of calming those around him. Jackson is the CEO of Pinnacle Bank in Elberton, Georgia, which was founded in 1934 and previously helmed by his grandfather and father. It's the kind of stubborn old-school

institution that prides itself in community banking. Their headquarters aren't located in a gleaming high-rise; they're next to
a Dollar Tree and an Ace Hardware. It's the kind of bank that
gives you a free toaster when you open a personal checking account.

When Jackson started working at Pinnacle in 1994, the
bank had $204 million in assets. When he became president in
2001, its assets were $311 million, and when Jackson took
over as CEO from his father in 2006, $414 million. Since then,
under Jackson's steady leadership, the bank's assets reached
$2 billion in 2021. In the meantime, he's created hundreds of
new jobs by expanding from three locations to twenty-four
across rural Georgia.

Most bankers who expand that fast are the kind of ruthless
leader you see in Hollywood movies, like Gordon Gekko from
*Wall Street*. But Jackson is a different kind of banker. I met him
through a dear friend about six years ago. Jackson had just
read my book *It's Not Just Who You Know*, and he invited me
to breakfast one day when he was passing through Denver for
business. I wasn't at my best that morning—not even close. I
had to take Caroline to the orthodontist, among a million other
things. Before I knew it, I was thirty minutes late for our breakfast and I texted Jackson, apologizing profusely.

"No problem, Tommy, I'll just grab another orange," he
wrote back.

Then I realized I had to pick up Tate from hockey practice,
so I texted Jackson again, apologizing for the further delay.
"No problem, Tommy," he said. "Take your time."

When I finally sat down at the restaurant, Jackson had been
waiting for over an hour. Any other CEO would have left,
deeply offended, after ten minutes. Yet here was Jackson, not
just any CEO but the chairman of the Georgia Bankers Asso-

ciation, sitting patiently and eating oranges as he waited for me to get my life together. That was the beginning of a beautiful friendship, and he later invited me to host a leadership retreat for his employees.

When I decided to break my own rule and invest money with Jackson, it wasn't just because he's more than quadrupled the size of Pinnacle Bank during his tenure as CEO. It was because of what I learned when I talked with his team. His people love him. Everyone from the managers to the bank tellers. They couldn't stop talking about Jackson. How he insists they take time off work to support their community, whether it's coaching Little League, teaching Sunday school, volunteering at the soup kitchen, or handing out water bottles at the local road race. How he understands the bank's purpose is more than taking deposits and making loans. As one story goes, Jackson was in his office when he noticed that a delivery truck had stalled in the bank's parking lot. The driver was tinkering with the engine but couldn't get it to start. If you've ever been to Georgia in August, you know how hot and humid it gets; Jackson brought the man water and asked how he could help.

"I called the service department and they'll come get me in a few hours," the driver replied.

"Great," Jackson said. "Do you want to come inside where it's air-conditioned and wait there?"

The man declined. He was delivering seafood to local restaurants, and the fish would spoil if it stayed out in the heat and thawed.

Then the CEO of one of the most successful banks in Georgia took off his suit jacket, rolled up his sleeves in the mid-nineties heat, and said, "Okay, well, let's load those fish into my car and we'll make the deliveries together." Jackson opened his trunk and began loading it with frozen cod, shrimp, sea bass, and swordfish, then spent the rest of his afternoon making deliveries to local restaurants. Who does that? Jackson McConnell does.

It wasn't until the COVID-19 pandemic that I truly understood the depth of Jackson's love for his employees. Like so many businesses, Pinnacle Bank struggled with how to service their customers when the lockdowns began. Banking was considered an essential business—people need to access their money, after all—but how could they stay open safely? In early April 2020, Jackson was on a conference call with some of the top bankers in the southern United States discussing their way forward. Quickly the conversation turned to layoffs.

"How many hourly employees are you laying off?" one banker asked.

"We're making the ones who don't show up use their sick days and vacation time," said another.

Reported one executive: "We're instituting unpaid furloughs and canceling health benefits until we know more."

I'll never forget the text message I received from Jackson while he was on that call: "I feel like an alien right now. All these banking executives are talking about taking away healthcare and laying off employees. These workers are real people! They've got children and spouses. They're scared just like everyone else. And now they're going to lose their jobs?!"

Jackson hung up and decided he would handle things differently. The next day, the Pinnacle Bank management team sent out a company-wide email: "First of all, our bank is fine," it read. "You don't have to worry about how we're doing financially. More important, your job is safe. Go take care of your family and make sure they are safe. Tell us what you're comfortable doing and what you're not comfortable doing, and we'll find a way forward together." Despite having a worker-first policy to ensure everyone's safety, Pinnacle managed to stay open safely during the worst days of the pandemic without laying off a single employee.

I want you to think for a moment: Who is on your yellow sticky note? Who is the Jackson McConnell in your life who invested in you, who inspired you to greatness, who was there to support you every step of the way? Now, who is on your blue sticky note? Who was the fan hogger who failed to lead, who always put themself first, who undermined your ascent instead of fueling it? Write these names down, then put them somewhere high up on your wall. Look at them every day. You might think there is a big difference between the people on your yellow and blue sticky notes, but that isn't always so. Sometimes it's only a moment of negative influence that gets burned in our minds forever.

That's why staying present in our interactions with others is so important. The best influencers aren't perfect all the time. They make mistakes. They get mad and say things they regret. But they are self-aware and humble enough to make it right. And no matter what, on the hottest, most miserable days, they point that fan toward others.

# Ask for Help

When Benjamin Franklin was serving in the Pennsylvania legislature, he developed an intense rivalry with another lawmaker. The more Franklin tried to court his vote, the nastier the man was. One day, Franklin decided to try another tactic. He approached his rival and asked if he could borrow a rare book from his collection. The man reluctantly agreed, and a week later Franklin returned the book along with a letter thanking him profusely. "When we next met in the House, he spoke to me (which he had never done before), and with great civility," Franklin later wrote in his autobiography. "And he ever afterward manifested a readiness to serve me on all occasions, so that we became great friends, and our friendship continued to his death."

It turns out that Ben Franklin was on to something, because researchers have been studying this phenomenon ever since. They even have a name for it: the Ben Franklin effect. Basically, theory goes, we like people more after helping them. It seems paradoxical, but studies confirm this again and again. Now, as you can probably guess, this phenomenon has its limits. If all you do is go around asking people to give you things, they are going to get annoyed. But when your actions are aligned with your intentions, when your request is genuinely heartfelt, people not only want to help you, but they are also *honored* to do so.

I am always asking people for help. It's practically my full-time job. For example, every week I call up a business leader and tell them about a disadvantaged kid I'm trying to sponsor for the Global Youth Leadership Academy.

"Will you help them?" I ask.

More times than not, the answer is yes. These are people I've come back to time and again, people who are honored that I would ask them to contribute to a good cause. These are folks I have developed beautifully authentic, humble, and vulnerable relationships with—largely by asking them to serve others. So many of my most cherished relationships began with asking them for help.

A few years ago, the National Leadership Academy celebrated its twentieth anniversary. During that time, we've relied heavily on volunteers, food donors, scholarship sponsors, and other benefactors. For the past twenty years, I've asked Chris Harr and Shawn Early at PepsiCo to donate all the beverages for NLA events. The answer has always been yes. I've asked Mark Miller, vice president of high-performance leadership at Chick-fil-A, to donate hundreds of meals. The answer has always been yes. I've asked Bill Graebel if his company can be the presenting sponsor of NLA. The answer has always been yes. I've asked Matt Lambert, general manager of the Country Club at Mirasol, to host our retreats and NLA fundraisers for scholarships. The answer has always been yes.

This chapter might seem paradoxical. Most of this book has been about learning to set aside your ego and serve others. Asking for help can seem self-serving. It can make you look like a taker. I get it. Except that psychological studies routinely show that providing support is just as important as receiving support. The go-it-alone mentality might seem like you aren't being burdensome, but it also leaves you, well, alone.

After my parents got divorced, my mom married a wonderful man named Lou, her childhood friend growing up in White Plains, New York. They've been married for over twenty-five years. Now, Lou, he's as old-school as you get. He served in the U.S. Army and then worked his way up the corporate ladder at an international dairy foods conglomerate until he became chief operating officer. He was the highest-ranking American in the organization and a total no-nonsense leader. Lou was the first to arrive and the last to leave—the type of man who has his employees' backs no matter what, but don't expect any hugs. The only thing he was more devoted to than his work was my mom. But, like so many in Lou's generation, he rarely asks for help. When we go out to dinner, Lou pays every time, no questions. When he has a friend in need, it's his job to help, no one else's. If he isn't sure what to do, you'll never know it, because Lou always has an answer.

About a year ago, Lou and my mom got into a minor accident while driving from their home in Florida to North Carolina. The repair would take a couple of weeks, so they rented a car and returned home while the fixes were made. Lou is in his late seventies, and I didn't want him driving alone for the better part of two days, so I made plans to fly to North Carolina, pick up the car, and drive it to my parents'. When Lou caught wind of the plan, he immediately took a taxi to the airport, flew to North Carolina, got the car, and drove twelve hours home, alone. He later thanked me for my generous offer, but his message was clear: He does not ask for help, even from family.

We lionize people like Lou—the last of a generation who fought fascism and then got to work making America the most prosperous country in the world. But those strong-and-silent-type values can also prevent us from honoring others. When I am faced with big life decisions, I ring up my mentors, Jerry Middel, Bill Graebel, Walt Rakowich, Frank DeAngelis, Scott Lynn, and others, to ask their advice. They deeply appreciate being relied upon in that way, and they are honored that I seek their counsel. I'm also not afraid to ask for help from people I barely know. I once met a guy named Joe Sanders at a dinner party. He runs a wonderful organization called Colorado Uplift, which fosters new generations of urban leaders by linking at-risk youth with mentors. At the time, my stepson, Anthony, was dealing with some anxiety while applying to the United States Military Academy. I knew that Joe was a retired Air Force colonel and the former director of the United States Air Force Academy's Center for Character and Leadership Development. I figured: Who better to counsel Anthony through this stressful period?

Out of the blue, I called up Joe and asked for help. "Joe, I know you're a busy man, but I literally cannot think of a better role model for Anthony. You're the caliber of man I want him to be one day, and I would be so appreciative if you took him out to coffee." Not only did Joe clear his calendar that Friday to meet with Anthony, but he called him every week during the application process. It was a big ask, and Joe was honored to help.

Think about the last time someone made an amazing introduction for you. If you're like most people, your instinct is to be humble and grateful and not come across as an opportunist. Except, great leaders understand that you should never let an important connection go to waste—not for your own benefit but for another person's.

To explain what I mean, let me tell you about a boy named Braidy, who attended our Global Youth Leadership Academy in Tuscany, Italy. We were on the bus one day when I noticed that Braidy was jamming out to his headphones. He had his eyes closed as he danced in his seat, having one of those transportive moments only music can provide. Curious, I edged into the seat next to him and listened, expecting to hear the likes of Drake, Taylor Swift, or Ed Sheeran. To my surprise, the song I heard bleeding out of his headphones was a song from the musical *The Book of Mormon*. As the song reached its crescendo, Braidy wasn't just mouthing the lyrics—he was belting them out. And he was good. *Very* good.

"Braidy," I said, tapping his shoulder. He seemed startled, as if I'd woken him up from a vivid dream. "You're an incredibly good singer. Where did you learn to sing like that?"

"It's just a hobby," he said sheepishly. "I didn't realize I was singing out loud."

"You could be on Broadway one day with pipes like that. Have you thought seriously about singing in musicals for a living?"

"I don't know. I'm probably not good enough."

Later that day we went truffle hunting at a centuries-old farm. Afterward, while feasting on our bounty, I asked Braidy to perform for the group. He knocked our socks off with a rendition of the opening number from *The 25th Annual Putnam County Spelling Bee*. It was his first time performing in front of an audience, but you never would have known it. He looked like he was born on that stage. The following year, Braidy won the part of Roger in his high school musical, *Rent*. It's the lead role, and it's very difficult—especially for a freshman. I took my family to see the show, and of course Braidy nailed the part.

One day during Braidy's sophomore year of high school, my literary agent, Michael Palgon, called to tell me about a new client he had signed: the Broadway star Robert Creighton. Bobby, as everyone calls him, is basically theater royalty, having starred in the likes of *The Lion King, The Mystery of Edwin Drood, Anything Goes, Chicago,* and *Chitty Chitty Bang Bang.* He's a genuine triple threat, meaning he excels at singing, dancing, and acting. Bobby was coming to Denver for a monthlong preview of the new Disney musical *Frozen.*

"You two should meet up," Michael suggested.

Now, I love Broadway. *Love* it. Meeting Bobby Creighton would have been a once-in-a-lifetime opportunity for me, but instead of using it to score tickets or a backstage pass, I reflected on my intentions and immediately thought of Braidy. I gave Bobby a ring, and here's how that first conversation went:

"Hi, Bobby, this is Tommy Spaulding. Our agent, Michael, thought we should get together. I was wondering if I could ask you for help. You see, I know a seventeen-year-old kid named Braidy . . ."

When I told Bobby the story, he immediately agreed to join me for a golf foursome with Braidy and his father, Scott. When the day arrived, I didn't tell Braidy whom we were golfing with. "Oh, my friend Bobby—you might know him," I said cryptically.

When Bobby walked into the clubhouse, he shook our hands and said, "So who's the future Broadway star that's golfing with me today?"

I would have paid a small fortune to see Braidy's expression immortalized in a painting. Bobby was his hero, and now he would be riding in a golf cart with him for eighteen holes. But believe it or not, watching those two stars bond wasn't the highlight of my afternoon. The highlight was riding with Scott, who was uncharacteristically quiet for three hours. He was watching his son chat animatedly with his idol. He saw a fire and passion in Braidy's face that he had never seen before.

"Tommy," he said to me with a grin, "my son is going to be a star, isn't he?" You know you've done something right when you hear that. Scott and Braidy will never forget that afternoon for the rest of their lives. And neither will I. Meanwhile, even though our relationship began with my asking for help, Bobby has become one of my closest friends on the planet.

What are some ways you can honor others by asking for their help? Here's a great place to start: Find a person with a skill set you admire and ask them to mentor you. Not long ago I was hired by my friend Mark Honnen to lead team-building exercises for his managers at his John Deere dealership. Afterward, we all went out for margaritas at a Mexican restaurant. I watched Mark, who normally is a very straitlaced and focused CEO, loosen his tie and banter with his employees. I thought about my own staff—I love and respect them, but I couldn't let loose with them the same way Mark did. A few days later, I picked up the phone and called him.

"Mark, could you help me?" I explained that I took myself too seriously, that I just wanted to hang out with my employees without it being weird. "I just want to be able to have fun at work from time to time," I admitted.

Mark instantly agreed, and he even thanked me. He was touched that I noticed how much work he put in to cultivating an inclusive work environment. Mark has helped me become a better boss and a better man ever since, and we've become close friends.

Asking for help doesn't just help us become better people; it helps us become more vulnerable in our day-to-day lives. So, think about it: Who are you asking for help from today? If your instinct is to say "No one," remember that sometimes the greatest compliment you can give another person is to honor them by asking for their help.

# PART V

# The Circle of Influence

# Eagles and Seagulls

When I'm not traveling the country, I make sure I'm with my family as much as possible. Every year I pledge to spend more time at home, but somehow work gets in the way. From all the leadership speeches, trainings, and corporate retreats to my trips with the National Leadership and Global Youth Leadership academies, it seems I'm always on a plane somewhere. During the summer of 2021, when Anthony left for college at West Point, it hit me how little time we have with our kids before they leave the nest. When Tate received his first hockey prep school offer in eighth grade, from a school across the country no less, it hit me even harder.

When I realized that Caroline might soon be our only child left in the house, I wanted to spend as much time as I could with her. Like any teenager, she's not always wild about that idea, but occasionally she lets me tuck her in at bedtime. One evening, I kissed her good night as I always do, but something seemed a little off. For the past few days, she had seemed quieter than usual.

"Is something wrong, honey?" I asked. "Do you want to talk about it?"

"Daddy, I'm having trouble fitting in at school."

At first, I had trouble wrapping my head around that idea. I've always thought of Caroline as the popular girl. She's very outgoing. In middle school, she played basketball, won the role of Mary Poppins in the school musical, and finished at the top of her class. She's heavily involved in many organizations at her high school. Caroline charmed people so effortlessly with her poise and kindness that I never once thought she would have problems making friends.

Caroline explained that things started changing after she turned sixteen. Her friends began throwing parties with alcohol. She had no interest in any of that. Her idea of a fun Saturday night was offering to babysit or volunteering at a community service event. Instead of partying over summer vacation, she preferred to go to Bible camp. Caroline explained that while adults saw a fine young woman with impeccable values, some of her classmates saw a Goody Two-shoes.

I sometimes have trouble relating to my daughter. She is everything I wasn't when I was her age. She's brilliant, articulate, and humble. The leadership skills I've spent decades learning come so naturally to her. While Tate is a hurricane of energy who lives on the ice and inspires his teammates to play as hard as they possibly can, and Anthony is a natural-born leader who has pledged a life of sacrifice for his country, Caroline's influence is quieter, more steadfast, and embodied by the effortlessly good decisions she makes every single day. I sometimes fear she is too smart to benefit from any advice I could possibly give her.

But then the right words miraculously came to me. "Honey, have I ever told you about the eagles and the seagulls?" I asked.

Caroline shook her head.

"Well, seagulls are everywhere. There's millions and millions of them in the world. They hang out on the beach, in parks, at the dump. You can hear them a mile away. They're always grooming themselves and scavenging for food. They never fly above a hundred feet in the air. There's nothing wrong with seagulls, but you see them so often you don't even think about them. Eagles, on the other hand, are rare. They soar as high as airplanes. They can spot a tiny fish from hundreds of feet up. If you're lucky enough to see an eagle, you stop what you're doing and watch it in awe.

"Do you know which you are, honey?"

Caroline smiled faintly but still looked skeptical.

"Do you remember a few years ago when I asked if you wanted to go to Disney World for vacation? You said you would rather help build homes for the poor in Mexico. That's not what seagulls do."

Then she smiled a little wider.

"Every Christmas Day, when all your friends are opening their presents, you wrap sandwiches. Then you drag us to Costco so you can buy wool socks. Then we spend all day delivering sandwiches and socks to homeless people. That's not what seagulls do."

Now she was really smiling.

"Honey, I've dedicated my career to helping seagulls turn into eagles. You're one of the rare young ladies who's been an eagle from the day you were born."

I thought about that conversation for a long time afterward. The truth is, I spent the first thirty years of my life as a seagull. As I've written about before, when I was growing up in Suffern, New York, I struggled academically because of undiagnosed dyslexia. I was a fixture of the resource room because of my learning challenges. I had a stubborn lisp. I went to summer school all four years. I fell through the cracks. Yet because I was a Boy Scout and an altar boy and a good kid, my teachers let me squeak by even though I could barely read or solve basic math problems. The only one who commented on my struggles was my typing instructor, Ms. Dizzini, who couldn't understand why I mixed up letters all the time. "I guess you're just stupid, Tommy," she finally said, exasperated.

At the end of each week, my mom would sit me down at the kitchen table and ask: "What did you accomplish this week? What grades did you get? What chores did you get done?" My mom loved me dearly and was proud of my accomplishments, but in my insecure way, I sometimes felt I had to earn her love. I was constantly compared to my cousins, who excelled in sports and went on to great schools and great careers. With every failed test, every summer spent in a classroom, I felt more like the family failure. But I learned to mask that shame with sheer drive and ambition. I resolved that I'd prove to the world that I could be successful. I swore that one day I would be worth more money than all my cousins combined. Shamefully, this would remain my yardstick for success for more than a decade. I was addicted to achievements and success.

Even though I graduated from high school with a 2.0 GPA and bottom-ninetieth-percentile SAT scores, I achieved. I was elected senior class president. I performed the morning announcements, painstakingly memorizing each word so I would not stumble while reading. I was elected student ambassador. I became the youngest Eagle Scout in the history of my troop. I was the starting placekicker on the varsity football team. I sang in the school musicals and was captain of the ski racing team. I was a state and national DECA champion in entrepreneurship. I was president of Students Against Drunk Driving. I volunteered at my local church while also working part time at McDonald's and Domino's. I racked up so many achievements that I was voted "Did Most for Suffern High School" in the yearbook superlatives.

Every club presidency, every award, every accomplishment only fed my addiction to achieve, and this pursuit of recognition continued in college. Yet my grades were still abysmal. I failed Math 1065—basic algebra—six times. I attended summer classes because I didn't have enough credits. I like to joke that if you add together my high school and college GPAs, I graduated with a 4.0.

I had to keep feeding my achievement addiction. I went to business school in Australia and excelled. Instead of taking the job I really wanted after graduation—working for *National Geographic*—I took the job that offered me the biggest signing bonus and the biggest salary: Lotus Development (IBM) in Boston. By the time I turned thirty, I was a top salesman living in a million-dollar condo in the South End. I had traveled to more than eighty countries and lived in Europe, Asia, and Australia. I had checked every box, won every award. I had even achieved my goal of being worth more than all my cousins put together. And yet, deep down, I still felt like the resource room kid with dyslexia and a stutter. I still heard Ms. Dizzini's words echoing in my mind: *"I guess you're just stupid, Tommy."* No award, no salary, no title could fill that hole in my heart.

As I related in my first book, my moment of clarity came at a sales conference in 1999 at the Walt Disney World Swan and Dolphin Resort. The vice president of sales at Lotus Development stood onstage screaming, "We want more market share! More market share means you make more money!" Dollar bills rained like confetti as he pounded the lectern, and I watched as my colleagues pushed and shoved and hoarded the bills like children grubbing for piñata candy. When I returned home, I took a hard look at my motivations. I achieved for my own sense of pride, not because I wanted to help and influence others. I traveled not to learn about the world and other cultures but to show off all the stamps in my passport. I made money not to start a family or donate to worthy causes but in a vain attempt to prove that I wasn't stupid. I was thirty, depressed, and alone. Instead of building a life of meaning, I had spent ten years accumulating bullet points on a résumé. I was just another seagull picking at scraps. It had all been about me and the insecure hole in my heart.

And then it hit me. The only time I had been truly, unequivocally happy was when I toured the world as a teenager with Up with People. Back then, I had no money or career. I just wanted to help bring the world together. By learning to love and serve others, I had learned to love and serve myself. Somewhere along the way I had forgotten that lesson.

So I did something crazy. I quit my job, sold my condo in Boston, packed up my car, and drove to Denver, Colorado, to rejoin the organization that had changed my life. When I was thirty-five, I married Jill, who taught me the meaning of unconditional love. She loved me poor, and she loved me wealthy. She loved me in skinny jeans and in fat pants. Jill didn't care about my résumé or my awards. All she cared about was that I woke up each morning determined to learn something new and become a better person. When I left Up with People, I exhausted my savings to start a nonprofit called Leader's Challenge, which later became the National Leadership Academy. My goal was to serve young people like me who had fallen through the cracks.

In the twenty years since, we've had more than ten thousand kids participate in our National Leadership and Global Youth Leadership academies. With every successful graduation, the big hole in my heart is partially plugged. Shifting my heart and dedicating my life to serving others has been one of the greatest decisions I've ever made. Serving others still does not come as naturally to me as it does to eagles like Caroline. I still have challenges that hinder my ability to live a life of positive influence. I get angry and resentful too easily. I am slow to forgive. I can be selfish. But I do wake up every day and try to be better. My wife reminds me often that she truly appreciates my hard work to become the best man I can be.

And along the way I've learned the single most important rule of influence, which we're going to explore extensively in this section: *You can't love and positively influence the lives of others unless you love and positively influence yourself.*

# The Final *I* of Influence

get it. You're probably thinking: *Another* i *of influence?*
*Didn't we already get through those?*

It's true. We've discussed the three critical elements—
interest, investment, and intent—of positive influence. But
there's one last *i* to discuss, and in many ways it's the most
crucial. It has everything to do with the sentence you just read:
You can't love and positively influence the lives of others until
you love and positively influence yourself.

Are you ready for it? The final *i* of influence is . . . I. As in
*me. Myself. I.*

You can't love and positively influence the lives of others
until you love and learn to care for yourself. It took me thirty
long years to figure this out, and my life has never been the
same since.

Funny thing, I've been on thousands of flights in my life to
deliver speeches about leadership, but I never realized that one
of the most important leadership lessons was staring me in the
face every time I boarded a plane. See, before takeoff, you
watch the safety video while the flight attendants point out the
emergency exits. You've heard it a million times: "In case of a

cabin pressure emergency, put on your own mask first before assisting others." If, during an emergency, you focus only on helping others, you'll soon pass out from lack of oxygen. Instead, as the flight attendants tell us, you need to ensure your own safety before turning your attention to the people next to you. It's a simple concept that also speaks to the heart of influence: You can assist far more people in the long run by taking care of yourself first.

What if we applied that lesson to life? What if we spent a little more time prioritizing our own needs so that we might better serve others in the future? It might sound counterintuitive and even selfish, but imagine a life in which you have more time, more happiness, and more energy to make a greater impact on the lives of others.

The first step in prioritizing your own needs begins with having gratitude. It's being grateful for the blessings in your life. For example, I'm grateful that I have a beautiful, healthy family. I'm grateful that no matter what trials we endure, nothing will ever come between us. I'm grateful that I grew up with two loving parents, who are now loving grandparents. You get the idea. Being grateful means thinking not about what you aren't but about what you *are*. It's thinking about what you *have* rather than about what you don't have. When you tell the people who are most important to you how much you love them and how grateful you are for their qualities, it softens their hearts as well as your own. Being grateful for the people you love most is the foundation for ensuring that they stay in your life forever, and that your bonds will only continue to deepen.

When you are grateful for life's blessings, you might realize how little time you are devoting to them. Having an attitude of gratitude not only gives us a more positive outlook on life, it gives us better perspective. A while back I took out a piece of paper and wrote down my most important commitments. My faith, my family, my friends, and my work were at the top. But then I went on to list twenty-two other obligations I had crammed into my life, including ministry work, civic clubs, and serving on nonprofit boards and advisory committees. These activities gave me a sense of contribution. They gave me great pride. Except I was stretching myself too thin, clinging to good things in my life that were preventing me from focusing on the great. I felt as if I were in my twenties all over again, accumulating achievements to mask my deepest insecurities. These were great and noble causes, but I simply did not have time for all of them.

One day I heard a man named Bob Doll say something that completely changed my thinking. After decades of working at firms such as BlackRock, Merrill Lynch, and OppenheimerFunds, Bob explained that when it comes to business, sometimes you have to "focus on the best at the expense of the good." He was referring to forward-thinking leaders who have to make tough choices, such as reinventing a successful business model to prepare for a future market, but I realized that the same idea can apply to our lives. I needed to let go of some of the "good" in my life so I could devote myself to what I was truly best at.

Then I remembered what Jill once said to me: "Sometimes I feel that everyone is getting the best of Tommy Spaulding except our family." So I did something a younger version of myself would never have done. I picked up the phone and called nearly all these boards, clubs, and committees and politely resigned. I needed time to refocus and recalibrate my priorities, I said. I was masquerading as a leader who did not have time to lead, and I needed to devote time to being a better husband, father, friend, and leadership coach. These were the areas where I could make the biggest difference in the world. I braced for the worst, ready to be accused of betrayal, dereliction, disloyalty—or worse. Instead, every single one of those organizations accepted my resignation with grace and appreciation. They said they respected my decision and wished me the best. Some of the folks I talked to said I had inspired them to sacrifice some of their own obligations to make room for what mattered most.

When I woke up the next day, it was as though someone had lifted a cement truck off my shoulders. Weirdly enough, I had never felt more like a leader than when I made those twenty-two calls and stepped down from those leadership positions. Jill and I have a saying we live by: "If everything is important, then nothing is." I've learned over the years that leaders need to be ruthlessly intentional with their time and their resources. They need to block and tackle tasks and to-dos so they can focus on what is most important: influencing the lives of others.

Way back in 1938, researchers at Harvard University wanted to figure out the key to a happy, healthy life. They followed 268 Harvard sophomores, tracking everything from their exercise habits to their careers to their marriages. Among the original subjects were President John F. Kennedy and the famed *Washington Post* editor Ben Bradlee. Amazingly, the study followed these Harvard students for eight decades and continues to this day, though only a handful are still alive. The study later expanded to include the subjects' children and grandchildren.

So, after eighty years, what did the study find was the secret to a long, healthy life? Here's what the director of the study, Robert Waldinger, had to say in 2015:

> When we gathered everything we knew about [the participants] about at age fifty, it wasn't their middle-age cholesterol levels that predicted how they were going to grow old. It was how satisfied they were in their relationships. The people who were the most satisfied in their relationships at age fifty were the healthiest at age eighty.

That's right, the single most important factor in living a healthy life wasn't diet or meditation or exercise. It was building lasting bonds with others. As another lead researcher explained: "The key to healthy aging is relationships, relationships, relationships."

Think about that for a second. You can treat your body like a temple, eat all the right foods, never smoke or drink alcohol, and kick your butt on the Peloton bike every day, but if you don't form meaningful relationships—if you don't lead a life of positive influence—it's all for nothing. This, at its heart, is the circle of influence. Relationships, relationships, relationships. They're the key to a happy life, and for too long I had been neglecting mine.

All of us are fully capable of forming and investing in new relationships. It just takes intentional effort. One day it hit me—I had closed myself off from so many wonderful people because I was traveling to twenty cities a month, my weight was fluctuating like a yo-yo, my stress level was through the roof. So I wrote down the names of six peers who had influenced me greatly, leaders who I believe are great men of faith,

husbands, fathers, and heart-led leaders. They were scattered
all over the country, from Iowa to Texas to Washington, D.C.,
to Georgia. What if we started meeting? Even though they had
never spent time with one another, I knew we could build something special. We could meet every month and "do life" together. It would be the rock in my calendar that I so desperately
craved, a refuge where my closest peers could cry and laugh
and grow together.

All six agreed instantly. We met up for the first time in Des
Moines, Iowa, at a steak house called 801 Chophouse. I went
around the table and introduced each person in turn—not by
their professional accomplishments but by how they had influenced me. There was Craig, father of six, including two adopted
from Ethiopia. He had taken my family to Mexico to build
homes and learn the value of giving back to those who were
less fortunate. "Craig is the greatest father I know," I explained
to the group. "I try to be like him every day." Then I introduced
Chase, a senior leader at Chick-fil-A in his early thirties who'd
attended my leadership retreat a few years earlier. "Meet
Chase," I told the group. "He might be twenty years younger
than us, but I've never met someone who embodies heart-led
leadership like him."

"Meet Brian," I continued. "There is not a more genuine
guy in the world than Brian. He has taught me to be a better
leader and a better man." Around and around I went, laying
out how much each of these leaders meant to me, how much I
loved them, and how much more I had to learn from them. We
spent hours talking and laughing and going deep, polishing off
a bottle of bourbon in the process. Then we retreated to the
lobby of our hotel and talked into the early hours of the morning. The seven of us were almost strangers when we arrived in

Des Moines, but we left as something entirely different. Not friends but brothers. We've met pretty much every month ever since.

We call our forum Iron Works, from one of my favorite proverbs: "As iron sharpens iron, so one person sharpens another" (Proverbs 27:17). Each month we fly to a different city, have dinner, open some bourbon, and talk about things that make us uncomfortable. *Where are you in your marriage? Where are you in your life? Your career? Your faith? Your family? How good have you been to your spouse? How good have you been to yourself?* We never stop challenging ourselves to be better in every possible way. We don't talk football or hockey or politics or other superficial matters. Our monthly meetups have become like a lighthouse in a storming sea, keeping us on course when life gets too much for one person to handle.

I've learned two big, life-changing lessons from Iron Works. The first: It's good to be self-interested. I hate how that term has become a synonym for "selfish." For being a jerk. My community of forum-mates has shown me that being self-interested does not mean being self-serving. Every month, my fellow Iron Works members grill me about what new thing I've learned about myself. About what qualities I need to work on to become a better father, husband, and leader. About what commitments I've shed so I can better focus on what I do best. But *you cannot love and serve others until you love and serve yourself.* That has become the motto of our Iron Works forum.

Second, I've learned the value of genuine conversation. I'm not talking about getting together with the guys or the gals to watch the game or the latest Netflix hit. I'm talking about challenging the most important people in your life to be honest about their problems, their marriages, their anxieties, their fears—whatever they avoid talking about. Make a habit of gently broaching these difficult topics. If that makes you squeamish, just know that science backs me up on this one. In one prominent study, researchers asked volunteers to wear a recording device for a few days. After categorizing each taped conversation as either "trivial small talk" or "substantive discussion," the researchers gave the participants well-being assessments to determine their overall happiness levels. Sure enough, the most contented people spent 25 percent less time alone. Moreover, they had twice as many substantive discussions and just one-third as much small talk as the unhappiest participants. "Our results raise the interesting possibility that happiness can be increased by facilitating substantive conversations," the study concluded.

What's your version of Iron Works? Do you have a core group of men and women who make you stronger? You might have your golf partners, poker buddies, work friends, book group, Bible study, and other spheres of your life that rarely intersect. Pick five or six of these people you respect most, the relationships that you depend on, and start your own forum. Set a standing date, maybe only a few times per year, to "do life" together away from the ballpark, the bar, and the other fragile scaffolding that sustains so many friendships. Make yourself vulnerable and surround yourself with others who are willing to do the same. Strive to fill your stadium with eighty thousand people whose lives you have positively influenced, but never forget that your number one fan should always be *you*.

# 10xing Your Influence

A few weeks before I started writing this book, I asked my friends what they thought of my ideas. Most were blown away when I asked them to picture walking into a stadium packed with eighty thousand people they had influenced throughout their lifetime. They had never thought about it that way before. A few even texted me days later to say they hadn't been able to look the same way at their co-workers, clients, or even random people they pass by every day. Had they been a good influence, they wondered? A bad one?

Then one day I told my friend Sean Lambert about my book idea. "What do you think?" I asked when I was done with my spiel.

Sean scratched his chin thoughtfully, then said: "No. I don't like it, Tommy."

I laughed reflexively, assuming he was joking. After all, I had spent more than two years thinking about this book. What kind of friend would say they didn't like my ideas? Except Sean wasn't smiling.

"I'm dead serious, Tommy. I don't like it. Only two or three people per day? Only eighty thousand in a lifetime? That's nothing! Why would you stop at eighty thousand people? Why not influence eight hundred thousand, or eight million? It sounds to me like eighty thousand is the bare minimum. From what you tell me, real influencers don't stop at two or three people per day. They ten-times that."

And then Sean walked away.

I stood there stunned, until it hit me: Sean was right. I was fixated on influencing 2.8 people per day—the minimum. I could sleepwalk through life and still influence the same number of people. I had never stopped to think what would happen if I truly made a point of practicing influence in the ways I've written about in this book.

Sean himself is a 10xer. He grew up in a modest home in Minneapolis, and like me, he struggled in school. He felt he lacked direction and purpose. He got a job as a bag boy at the local supermarket to pay the bills. One day, a co-worker named Dale invited him to a youth Bible study at the local church. The weekly meetings energized Sean like nothing he had ever experienced. Dale continued to invest in Sean, even inviting him to become a counselor at a summer camp teaching sixth graders about the Bible. It took some time, but Dale's investment paid off. Sean developed leadership skills he never thought he possessed. "I discovered the joy of serving others," he later wrote. "Dale told me years later that he had set a goal to influence one person's life each year, and in 1975 I was that one person." Sean was determined to be a difference maker like Dale, but he had a nagging thought: Instead of influencing one life each year, what if he could influence ten lives? Or a hundred? Or a thousand?

A few years later, Sean joined the outreach organization Youth with a Mission and traveled to Thailand, where he assisted thousands of Cambodian and Laotian war refugees and learned how to minister to people by addressing both their spiritual and practical needs. For the next decade he worked with YWAM in Los Angeles, mobilizing thousands of young people in short-term outreach programs. In 1990, he traveled with his young daughter, Andrea, and seventeen other YWAM staff to Tijuana, Mexico, to build a house for an impoverished family. As Sean hammered and painted in the burning heat, Andrea wandered over to an abandoned bus. A homeless family was living inside it, and she quickly made friends with a set of young twin sisters. The next day, she asked her father a question that would radically change his life and the lives of many others:

"Daddy, are you going to build a house for the bus people too?"

The question echoed in Sean's heart for the rest of the trip. It continued to echo when they returned to Los Angeles. He thought back to his mentor Dale, who pledged to influence one person per year. Sean had built one home for one poor family, but that struck him as the bare minimum. What was stopping him from building two, six, or ten more?

Sean couldn't get the "bus people" out of his thoughts. So eight weeks later he returned to Tijuana with a team of twenty high school students and built the bus family a home. The experience inspired him to start a new ministry of YWAM called Homes for Hope, devoted to building homes for the poor. There were plenty of ups and downs, but they built twelve houses over the next twelve months. The next year they built twenty-four. It took twelve years to reach one thousand homes built, but only four more to reach two thousand. By the end of 2022 they will pass 7,500 homes built, engaging 140,000 Homes for Hope volunteers and providing shelter for 37,500 people in twenty-five countries.

Here's the critical point about 10xers like Sean: They don't

10x their number of commitments. As we saw in the previous chapter, that kind of thinking is unsustainable and a disservice to your own relationships and your own happiness. Rather, they 10x the one thing they're best in the world at, the one thing that can change the most lives. For Sean, it's building homes for the poor. For me, it's inspiring and teaching others to be heart-led leaders, and to have a positive influence on the lives of others.

When you aggressively narrow your scope of influence, there is no limit to how much you can achieve. Take my friend Matthew Kelly, for instance. Born and raised in Sydney, Australia, Matthew was the fourth of eight boys. He was raised a committed Catholic, but he became restless and discontented in his faith, and his attention drifted to starting a business. A natural communicator, he discovered he had a gift for public speaking. In college, he delivered motivational speeches and quickly built a devoted following. By the time he was twenty, Matthew was a full-time speaker delivering some 250 speeches per year. Next came the self-help books—a lot of them. Now, I published three books by the time I turned fifty-three. I thought that was a neat achievement until I found out that Matthew Kelly had published that many before he turned twenty-five. He's since published about two dozen more, which have collectively sold more than fifty million copies in over thirty languages. At some point you've probably heard his trademark phrase: "Become the best version of yourself."

By the time he hit his mid-thirties, Matthew was an extremely successful author and speaker. He had founded a management consulting firm that counted dozens of Fortune 500 companies as clients. But Matthew began to feel burned out. He had the books and the speeches and the consulting, but they were pulling him in three different directions. Matthew has the energy of a thousand suns, but he was using it to brighten a million planets. What if he could redirect that energy toward something he was truly passionate about? What if he could 10x his talents into a single purpose? Matthew's friends must have felt his ambivalence too, because one day they confronted him at home and staged an intervention. "Matthew," they said, "you're too talented to keep doing what you're doing. The self-help books, the consulting—that's all great. But that's not where your real purpose lies. You're not doing what matters most to you: helping your church."

Even though he had grown up a devout Catholic, Matthew had seen the church become consumed by scandals and flagging attendance. It was losing relevance to people like me, who were strong believers but had grown disenchanted with its direction. For years, Matthew realized, he had developed strategies for his corporate clients to improve employee engagement. Why had no one done the same for the Catholic Church? That day, Matthew decided he would cut back on the traveling and writing and laser-focus on helping Catholics rediscover their love of God. In 2009, he formed a nonprofit called Dynamic Catholic, with a mission to "re-energize the Catholic Church in America by developing world-class resources that inspire people to rediscover the genius of Catholicism." Matthew's first order of business was to commission a nationwide research study on engagement in the Catholic Church. The results were sobering and clear: The church needed to modernize. It needed to accept criticism and bring young people back into the fold.

And then Matthew got to work. He laid out a vision for the church and invited its leaders to join him. Of the fifteen thousand U.S. Catholic parishes, more than twelve thousand are now using at least one Dynamic Catholic program. His 2017 book, *Beautiful Hope,* included an essay from Pope Francis himself. In fact, it was because of Matthew that I reconnected with my own Catholic faith. After I mentioned to him that I was having trouble returning to the church, he invited me to speak at Dynamic Catholic's headquarters in Cincinnati. I spent the evening with his amazing staff—mainly young people, like Jack Beers, who were fired up to help Catholics and their parishes become the best versions of themselves. They inspired me to come to terms with why I had strayed from the church, and why I so desperately wanted to return again.

Let me tell you the most beautiful part about being a 10xer. Sure, there are influencers like Sean Lambert who are literally saving lives. There are influencers like Matthew Kelly who are single-handedly reforming the oldest institution in the world. But most 10xers are living much quieter lives. Take my close friend Lisa Haselden, for example. You could've forgiven her if she hadn't turned out to be a very nice person. Her father was an alcoholic who fell out of her life when she was a teenager. She hasn't seen him in over two decades. Lisa's mother, meanwhile, struggled with mental illness and was unable to parent. She was verbally abusive toward Lisa for her entire childhood. The situation was so heartbreaking that Lisa never learned to call her mother Mom. She was just Sharon. I've worked with thousands of kids in my life, and I know how hard it is to have a normal adulthood when your parents are that screwed up. It can take years or decades of therapy to build empathy and regain faith in other people.

Lisa, however, is a 10xer. When she was in her twenties, she met her soulmate, Byron, and one of the first things they did as a married couple was to buy a house for the person Lisa could never call Mom. When my wife's father, Ernie, passed away a few years ago, Lisa made the two-hour trip to his funeral despite barely having known the man. When our friend Mark

Burke died suddenly, Lisa made caring for his family her full-time job. She even helped Mark's son buy an engagement ring so he could propose to his girlfriend. I once asked her how she could be such a giver after her awful childhood. She said simply, "I was born in a very deep hole, Tommy, but I'm climbing my way out by serving as many people as I can. I do it for myself as much as I do it for them."

Lisa is the most relentless everyday influencer I know, and she is living proof that 10xers don't have to be celebrities with millions of social media followers. They don't have to reform two-thousand-year-old institutions, build hundreds of homes for the poor, or run multinational nonprofits. Lisa's version of 10xing is simply waking up in the morning and asking herself, "Who in my community can I serve today?"

Until now, I've wanted you to think about the number eighty thousand: the number of people the average person influences in their lifetime. But in a world full of average—in a world full of seagulls—what if you could be outstanding? Consider what living a life of 10x means for you. What is that single thing you do best that has the capacity to inspire others and change lives? How can you simplify your life so that you have the time, energy, and love to devote yourself to it?

For many years, I avoided these questions. I was content writing books and traveling the country giving speeches about leadership. I figured this was the best way I could positively influence the lives of others. But then a funny thing happened. I was at a hotel in Miami a few months after I finished the first draft of this book when I ran into none other than Sean Lambert at the pool.

When I mentioned I had just wrapped up *The Gift of Influence,* he frowned. "Hey, Tommy, I hope I didn't offend you that time I said I didn't like your idea. It's just that I think God put you on this earth to do more than sell books and coach businesspeople. I think that millions and millions of people should hear your message. What do you think is the best way you can do that?"

And then, once again, Sean walked away.

Truth is, I did know the best way I could 10x my influence, and I had been too scared to pursue it. I had understood my dream ever since I walked into the Suffern High School auditorium and watched Up with People perform thirty-five years earlier. That day I learned about the power of community, diversity, and music. When I joined that organization, I saw firsthand what happened when young people from every walk of life, from every corner of the globe, and from every race, ethnicity, and religion came together to build bridges of understanding.

After Sean challenged me for the second time, I realized I had to go back to my roots and return to the place where it all had begun. My decades of experience building two nonprofits and a leadership-training company would lead me right back to that high school auditorium, this time in charge of my own national leadership program for young people. I even knew exactly what I wanted to call our movement: Red, White, and YOU. My 10x goal is to reach every high school in America with a cast of kids who look, speak, and sing like Americans. Black, white, gay, straight, Catholic, atheist, liberal, conservative, country singers, and rappers—everyone will be welcome. We will teach students to love their country, love their classmates, and love themselves. We will inspire youth to appreciate the delicate freedoms they enjoy and to give back in any way they can. Red, White, and YOU will remind young Americans once more that it's not about what your country can do for you, but what you can do for your country. With a kick in the butt from my friend Sean, I finally decided to 10x my influence, and I can't wait for what's in store next.

What is your 10x dream? If your friends tossed you in a room and refused to let you out until you came up with an idea to supercharge your influence, what would it be? When you discover what that is, go out there and fill your stadium—and then fill another one. Fill ten more stadiums with screaming fans whose lives are ten times better because of the gift of your influence. In the process, something beautiful will happen: As I've learned time and again, when life deals you a bad hand, when you're at rock bottom, when you desperately need an eagle to soar in and give you a lift, you'll find ten stadiums full of people ready to return your gift of influence ten times over.

# Epilogue

## THREE QUESTIONS

Years ago, before I began writing this book, Jill and I attended a dinner party in Denver and sat next to a remarkable woman named Tina. We got to talking, and Tina explained that she worked at a hospice center caring for terminally ill cancer patients. When I asked Tina the most important thing she'd learned in her work, she paused for a few moments before explaining that many of her patients have no family left. She takes tremendous pride in bathing them, helping them dress, and tending to their medical needs. But her most important lesson came from listening to their stories and simply being a witness to their final days.

"The most important thing I've learned," Tina continued, "is the three questions my patients all ask: Was I loved? Did I love back? Did I make a contribution? These are the questions my patients ask me over and over. That is their legacy, and it's my job to learn as much as I can about their lives, reassure them, and bring them peace before they pass on. You have no idea how grateful I am to them. I can ask myself these questions now, while there is still time to make a difference."

For some reason, later that night, my mind drifted back to my freshman year at East Carolina University. I lived across the hall from a student named Steve, who grew up on the Outer Banks of North Carolina. A few years earlier, Steve and his buddies hopped on his boat for a weekend fishing trip. They motored a hundred miles offshore, past the continental shelf, where the ocean drops to more than a mile deep. At the end of a sweltering day, Steve pulled off his shirt and dived into the water headfirst. At that exact moment, on that exact swath of remote ocean, a giant sea turtle swam by. Steve slammed his head on its shell, instantly paralyzing him from the waist down. It was a freak accident, eerily similar to what happened to my friend Chad Harris, whom we met earlier in the book. Steve explained to me that he had come to terms with his incredible misfortune, but he couldn't help but wonder sometimes: "Why me?" When I was sitting on that Southwest Airlines plane, praying for it to crash, I thought the same thing: *Why me? Why am I so depressed? Why is everything going wrong for me? Why is my world falling apart?*

I've realized that most of us obsess over the "Why me?" question for our entire lives. It gnaws at our brains in our worst moments. Why does Anthony's father hate me? Why did my sub sandwich business fail? Why did God give me dyslexia? Why did He give me a lisp? Why did He put a sea turtle under that boat? We never get answers to these questions—we never will—and yet we agonize over the injustice of it all. It isn't until we are faced with death that we finally ask the three questions that matter. The three questions we can actually answer if we understand the influence we have on the lives of others.

Was I loved? Did I love back? Did I make a contribution?

Imagine being able to answer these questions before we are old men and old women, before our bodies fail us and we are left in the care of gentle souls like Tina. Instead of asking "Why me?" what if we went to bed each night softly repeating: "I am loved. I love back. I am making a contribution." How wonderful would that be?

On October 17, 2021, a few weeks after I finished the first draft of this book, I found myself asking another "Why?" question. I had just received the heartbreaking news that my cousin's daughter, Madelyn Nicpon, had died after choking during a hot-dog-eating contest raising money for charity. She was just twenty years old. It was a freak accident, one in a million.

*Why her?* I thought. *Oh God, why her?*

Madie grew up in my hometown of Suffern, New York, and was everything I was not at her age. She had a GPA north of 4.0; she was co-president of the National Honor Society and an all-star field hockey and lacrosse player. When she enrolled at Tufts University, she intended to enter pre-med and become a pediatrician. She was one of those rare individuals who excelled at everything she did and knew exactly what her purpose was in life. She was a true eagle.

A few days later, I flew to New York for the memorial service. I was expecting a fairly large crowd—her family, her high school and college friends, her lacrosse teammates, perhaps some coaches and teachers. What I saw nearly brought me to my knees. Thousands of people had descended on the Church of the Presentation in Saddle River, New Jersey. Bus after bus unloaded students from Tufts University who had made the two-hundred-mile journey from Boston to say goodbye to Madie—or Scooter, as they affectionately called her. Her high school classmates had flown in from colleges across the country to say goodbye. All told, more than five thousand people lined up outside that church to say goodbye. The priest who led the service said it was the largest crowd he had ever seen at a funeral.

During the memorial, people told stories about how Madie

always put others first. How she lifted others with her infectious laughter. How she volunteered with EMS and paramedics. How she twice traveled to Jamaica on missions to help orphans and children with disabilities. How she helped put children and their parents at ease at the pediatrician's office where she worked part time. In that moment, I was truly sitting in Madie's stadium, surrounded by thousands of strangers who loved her just as much as I did.

Then I learned something I'd never known about Madie. After needing a nerve graft following wisdom tooth surgery, she became a tireless advocate for organ donation. When Madie died, her body had been placed on life support so that her organs could be preserved. Her beautiful eyes gave sight to a blind patient. Her kidneys saved the lives of two women. Her tissue, lungs, bones, and nerves will change the lives of countless more. Madie lived only twenty short years, but her influence will quite literally live on.

I'll never know why Madie was taken from us so soon. But I do know one thing: She was never someone who asked *Why me?* After seeing bus after bus pull up to the memorial, after seeing the thousands of people who loved her and whom she loved back, after hearing the stories of how much she contributed and gave back to her community—I knew. I knew that she spent every day confident in the answers to Tina's three questions. *Was I loved? Did I love back? Did I make a contribution?* Her legacy will continue answering those questions for those who did not know her.

Madie's life is a testament to the indelible power of positive influence: how anyone—from junior high school teachers to hockey players to gang leaders to Catholic nuns to twenty-year-old college students to you, reading these words right now—can radically change lives if only we choose to. We can live a great life of influence by speaking less and listening more. By investing in the lives of others and expecting nothing in return. By helping our followers become more successful than ourselves. By choosing to love people who aren't in our immediate orbit. And above all else, by staying humble.

I can't answer the "Why me?" questions in life. You'll have to go elsewhere for that. But here is what I can promise you: By devoting yourself to a life of positive influence—by lifting others when they are down, embracing them when they are cast off, and acting when they are in need—I promise you won't have to ask yourself, "Was I loved? Did I love back? Did I make a contribution?"

You will already know.

# Acknowledgments

I've spent the last two years thinking more about whose eighty-thousand-seat stadium I will be in than about who will be cheering in mine. There are many special people that made *The Gift of Influence* into something I'm incredibly proud of. I'm cheering at the top of my lungs for the following people and their incredible gifts of influence:

To my ghostwriter, Nick Bromley, for your unwavering patience and professionalism.

To my literary agent, Michael Palgon, for bringing out the best on these pages, but also the best out of me.

To my publisher and dear friend, Tina Constable, for believing in what I have to share with the world.

To my editor, Derek Reed, and the entire Penguin Random House team. Thank you for pouring so much love and attention into this project.

To our Tommy Spaulding Leadership Institute team: Chelsey Panchot, Kaylee Hanson, Mitch McVicker, and Lauren O'Grady. The four of you make it ALL happen. Thank you for changing lives with me every day.

To my colleague and friend Catie Hargrove. Thank you for putting your heart and soul into our Heart-Led Leader retreats.

To my Iron Works Men's Forum. I love doing life with you, Brian Flegel, Chase Shaw, Jon Sefton, Doug Ecklund, Craig Porter, and Matt Fryar.

To my mentors Bill Graebel, Jerry Middel, Walt Rakowich, Steve Arterburn, Frank DeAngelis, and Scott Lynn. I am who I am today because of the six of you.

To all the donors and volunteers of the Ben Graebel National Leadership Academy and the Global Youth Leadership Academy. Thank you for helping change the hearts and minds of thousands of young leaders.

To Beth Sargent and my dear GM friends at FLCMAA and CMAA. Thank you for helping me bring heart-led leadership to the club industry.

To Corey Turer, Garry Dudley, Bobby Creighton, Lisa and Byron Haselden, Ted Trask, Scott Diggs, Joe Krenn, Chris Hennessy, Charlie Host, Matt Lambert, Chip Misch, Chris Kisch, Terry Adams, and Andy Newland. You are the best friends anyone could ask for.

To my parents, Tom and Angie Spaulding & Diane and Lou Marino, for your unconditional love and belief in me.

To my sisters, Lisa Marie and Michele Joy. Our grandfather was right. The three most important things in life are: family, family, and family.

To my wife, Jill. Thank you for the gift of your influence, for the gift of your love, and for being the best human being I know. Home is just another word for you.

To our children: Anthony, Caroline, and Tate. Your mother and I are incredibly blessed to watch the three of you soar like eagles.

And all the glory to my heavenly Father. "I can do all things through Christ who strengthens me" (Philippians 4:13).

# About the Author

TOMMY SPAULDING is the founder and president of the Tommy Spaulding Leadership Institute, a leadership development, speaking, training, and executive coaching firm based in Denver, Colorado. A world-renowned speaker on leadership, Spaulding has spoken to thousands of organizations, associations, educational institutions, and corporations around the globe. His first book, *It's Not Just Who You Know: Transform Your Life (and Your Organization) by Turning Colleagues and Contacts into Lasting, Genuine Relationships*, published by Penguin Random House in 2010, quickly climbed to the top of the *New York Times, Wall Street Journal*, and *USA Today* national bestseller lists. His second book, *The Heart-Led Leader*, published by Penguin Random House in 2015, is a *New York Times* and #1 *Wall Street Journal* national bestseller and was also listed on Inc.com's Top 100 Business Books. Spaulding rose to become the youngest president and CEO of the celebrated leadership organization Up with People. He is the founder and president of the Global Youth Leadership Academy and the National Leadership Academy, both highly acclaimed national high school leadership development organizations. Previously, Spaulding was the business partner sales manager at IBM/Lotus Development and a member of the Japan Exchange and Teaching (JET) program. He received a bachelor's degree in political science from East Carolina University (1992); an MBA degree from Bond University in Australia (1998), where he was a Rotary International Ambassadorial Scholar; and a master's degree in nonprofit management from Regis University

(2005). In 2006, Spaulding was awarded the Outstanding Alumni Award by East Carolina University, and in 2007, Spaulding received an honorary PhD in humanities from the Art Institute of Colorado. In 2012, Spaulding was named by *Meetings & Conventions* magazine as one of the 100 Most Favorite Speakers in the nation. Spaulding resides in Denver, Colorado, and Faribault, Minnesota, with his wife and children.

tommyspaulding.com

## About the Type

This book was set in Sabon, a typeface designed by the well-known German typographer Jan Tschichold (1902–74). Sabon's design is based upon the original letterforms of sixteenth-century French type designer Claude Garamond and was created specifically to be used for three sources: foundry type for hand composition, Linotype, and Monotype. Tschichold named his typeface for the famous Frankfurt typefounder Jacques Sabon (c. 1520–80).

New York Times bestselling author Tommy Spaulding shows you how looking inward–and leading with your heart–can transform your life. Authentic leaders, Spaulding says, live and lead from the heart. The values and principles that guide our lives and shape our ability to lead others are far more important than our titles, or our ability to crunch numbers, or the impressive postgraduate degrees we display on our walls.

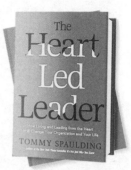

To effect true transformational change, heart-led leaders draw on the qualities of humility, vulnerability, transparency, empathy, and love. Illustrated with stories from Spaulding's own life, and from some of the exceptional leaders he has met and worked with over the years, The Heart-Led Leader unpacks what those qualities mean, talks about the eighteen-inch journey from the head to the heart–from our intellect to our emotions–and shows us how to incorporate them into our careers, into how we manage and lead others, and into how we live our lives.

"The Heart-Led Leader is an important book because it not only speaks about servant leadership but also is one of the first of its kind to connect this leadership philosophy to bottom-line results. And with his tear-jerking storytelling, Tommy Spaulding writes the book in a way that makes it hard to put down."
–Walt Rakowich, former CEO & president, Prologis

"In It's Not Just Who You Know, Tommy Spaulding delivers his ideas and life experiences in a way that can really help people achieve relationship excellence. This book should be required reading."
–Lee Cockerell, executive vice president (retired) of Walt Disney World Resort

**Investing unselfishly in the lives of others is the most important thing we can do for ourselves, our organizations, our communities, and our world.**

Tommy Spaulding, New York Times bestselling author, overcame enormous obstacles on his path to success, beginning with dyslexia, which hamstrung his academic career. What shaped and powered his extraordinary achievements in every area of his life were his relationships with people. In this compelling, story-driven narrative, Spaulding reveals the nuts and bolts behind turning casual contacts and chance encounters into opportunities to create authentic and lifelong relationships, both personal and professional.

# TOMMY SPAULDING **PROGRAMS**

LEADERSHIP *changing* LIVES

## KEYNOTES

Tommy Spaulding is a world-renowned leadership expert, *New York Times* bestselling author, and inspirational speaker. He speaks to over a hundred companies, associations, and audiences all over the world each year. Spaulding has humbly become one of the world's greatest storytellers. His messages of building authentic relationships, leading from the heart, and harnessing the power of positive influence leave audiences laughing, crying, and wanting to lead and live differently.

## TRAININGS

Tommy Spaulding offers trainings based on his *New York Times* bestselling books, customized to suit clients' needs and goals. The trainings can be done at your workplace or an off-site location. They are stimulating and geared for active participation by your staff. Participants will not only be inspired but leave with hearts filled with love and heads packed with the practical knowledge to put into action on a daily basis.

## BIKES TEAM-BUILDING

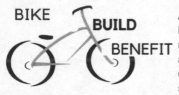

A team-building session designed around building a bicycle for a cause. Teams soon realize that they've built more than a bike. They've built a stronger team and made a lasting impact in a child's life. This is a half-day, hands-on, intensive training and team-building experience suitable for thirty to three hundred participants.

## WEBINARS

Tommy Spaulding is offering fully customized, live or prerecorded, online webinars to teach and inspire organizations and teams to be Heart-Led Leaders in the face of today's challenges. Based on his *New York Times* bestselling books, Spaulding will personalize your webinar experience with relevant stories and leadership lessons to encourage your employees, teams, and leaders with practical knowledge to put into action to help your organization move forward and succeed in building a winning culture.

TO LEARN MORE ABOUT TOMMY SPAULDING PROGRAMS, VISIT:

### TOMMYSPAULDING.COM

# HEART-LED LEADER
## RETREATS

Defining our leadership philosophy is one of the most critical decisions we make as a leader. It is one thing to read about becoming a heart-led leader, but it is another to actually become one. Heart-Led Leader Retreats teach and inspire participants to lead and serve others in a results-based way. Attendees will gain life-changing insight and training from world-renowned thought leaders, CEOs, and business experts in an intimate country club or resort setting, over three days and two nights, with twenty-five participants. Participants will dive deep and build meaningful and lasting relationships as well as learn how not only to become a heart-led leader but to live and lead a life of positive influence on the lives of others. To register for this year's retreats, please visit tommyspaulding.com/retreats.

"We've been sending twelve rising to senior leaders each year to Tommy's Heart-Led Leader Retreats and the results have been outstanding. In ten years' time, that would make 120 of our leaders championing what makes Graebel's culture so unique—a culture of love and service toward all our employees and our customers."

—Bill Graebel
CEO & president, Graebel Relocation

"I not only have attended one Heart-Led Leader Retreat but have participated in two. And both times left me recommitting myself to leading my team and our clients with a servant's heart. I am a different leader today because of these two retreat experiences."

—Jayne Hladio
Senior VP, U.S. Bank Wealth Management

Honesty
Purpose Trust Character
Transparency Authenticity
Encouragement Love Vulnerability Honesty
Generosity Passion Empathy
Empathy Results Transparency
Self Awareness Purpose
Humility Empathy Trust
Authenticity Passion Love
Encouragement Trust
Character

Register online at www.tommyspaulding.com

## GLOBAL YOUTH LEADERSHIP ACADEMY

Founded in 2002, Global Youth Leadership Academy (GYLA) is a world-class educational and experiential learning program that provides high school students with leadership training, global and cultural awareness, and a commitment to heart-led leadership.

Each summer, fifty students from across the globe visit select international cities for a week and participate in a variety of educational and leadership development programs. Students develop lifelong friendships with their peers from around the world, learn from renowned leadership speakers & staff, participate in team-building exercises, and experience unique cultural adventures. GYLA's mission is to develop the next generation of heart-led leaders.

**For more information, please visit our website:**
**www.globalyouthleadershipacademy.com**

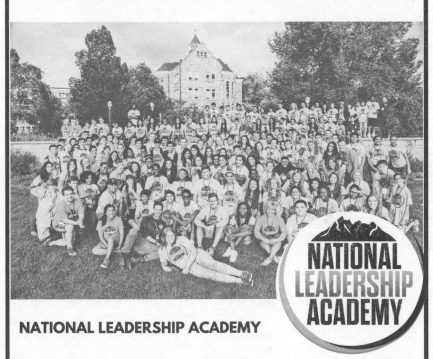

## NATIONAL LEADERSHIP ACADEMY

Since 2000, the National Leadership Academy (NLA), a high school youth leadership program, has inspired thousands of young leaders across America to become tomorrow's servant leaders.

National Leadership Academy develops and equips young people with the skills and confidence to be heart-led leaders. Our mission is to create civic- and service-minded young leaders by developing their leadership skills and heart for serving others. Our vision is to spark students into action in the hope that they take what they learn at NLA back to their schools and communities.

In our intensive four-day summer academy held at a private university in Denver, CO, students are mentored and taught by world-class leaders, engage in local community service projects, are challenged with outdoor team-building exercises, and develop lasting relationships with students from across the country. Student participants come away with lifelong skills in leadership training, communication, and service learning.

- To nominate a high school student or enroll, please visit our website: www.nationalleadershipacademy.org
- National Leadership Academy is a 501(c)(3) nonprofit program of the Tommy Spaulding Leadership Institute.